RICHARD S.B

URBAN PLANNING IN PLANET EARTH'S TRAGEDY OF THE COMMONS

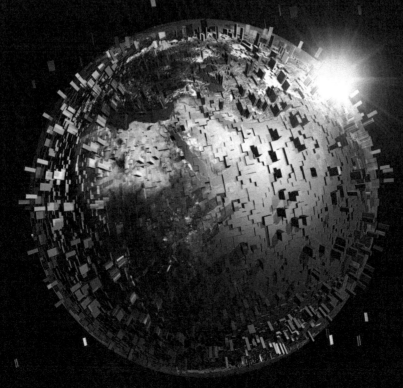

Urban Planning in Planet Earth's Tragedy of the Commons

iUniverse books may be ordered through booksellers or by contacting:

iUniverse
1663 Liberty Drive
Bloomington, IN 47403
www.iuniverse.com
1-800-Authors (1-800-288-4677)

ISBN: 978-1-5320-7910-8 (sc)
ISBN: 978-1-5320-7911-5 (e)

Library of Congress Control Number: 2019911237

Print information available on the last page.

iUniverse rev. date: 10/02/2019

This book is dedicated to:

my grandson: Garrett

and my seven step-grandchildren:

Katrina, Dan, Ben, August, Annalee, Thea, and Zane

and my two step great-grandchildren: Anna and Kloe

I fervently hope that 30 years from now global natural conditions will leave all of them healthy and free from air and water pollution, hurricanes, tornadoes, wild fires, infested agriculture, excessive heat, environmental disease and loss of biodiversity.

Contents

About the Author

Richard Stuart Bolan has a sixty-year career in urban planning. He graduated from Yale in civil engineering and from MIT with a master's degree in city and regional planning. He earned a PhD from New York University, majoring in urban planning and political science. He was a practitioner for ten years before joining the faculty at Boston College in 1967. While there, he served as editor for the *Journal of the American Institute of Planners*. In 1985, he moved to the Humphrey School of Public Affairs at the University of Minnesota. In 1990, he became involved in working in the countries of Central and Eastern Europe as they moved from Soviet-style communism to democratic, private-economy societies. His scholarly focus has been on planning theory and philosophy, and his most recent publications include *Urban Planning's Philosophical Entanglements: The Rugged, Dialectical Path from Knowledge to Action* (Routledge 2017).

Acknowledgments

While graduate trained in urban planning, I spent much time teaching environmental planning, a logical focus since my early study of civil engineering. Yet I came to learn that our approach to environmental planning was seriously deficient because of our lack of ability to bring economics, political science, and other social sciences into the environmental-planning process. The focus on environmental science was preventing us from fully understanding and adopting actions that would move us toward solving our current and local climate challenge and environmental damage.

The first author who gave me serious concern was Sheldon Wolin, a political scientist whose 2008 book, *Democracy Incorporated: Managed Democracy and the Specter of Inverted Totalitarianism*, provided the first hint that the corporate domain was really moving the world away from democracy. Another author who really accelerated my concern was Barry Lynn, a journalist whose 2010 book, *Cornered: The New Monopoly Capitalism and the Economics of Destruction*, highlighted the perils of oligopoly that had been moving dominantly since the 1980s. This book was also facing the economic downturn of 2008–2012. These two works highlighted how our ability in environmental planning was being diminished by the global corporate oligopoly. In effect, reading those two books really pushed me to begin work on this book.

From this, I am also indebted to several other authors who greatly helped my understanding of the Tragedy of the Commons. Jane Mayer's book *Dark Money: The Hidden History of the Billionaires behind the Rise of the Radical Right* is a *New York Times* best seller that illustrates how the use of money shapes the behavior of businesspeople and politicians—not just money earned by working but also inherited money and superfluous exchanges often under less-than-legal circumstances.

Other works have also helped in bringing my concern for urban planning to meet the earth's climate challenges. They include the following: Saaskia Sassen, *Cities in a World Economy*, fourth edition (2012); Robert Kuttner, *Can Democracy Survive Global Capitalism?* (2018); William Domhoff, *Who Rules America? The Triumph of the Corporate Rich* (2014); Martin Gilens, *Affluence and Influence: Economic Inequality and Political Power in America* (2012); Tim Jackson, *Prosperity without Growth: Foundations for the Economy of Tomorrow*, second edition (2018); Ian Gough, *Heat, Greed and Human Need: Climate Change, Capitalism and Sustainable Well Being* (2017); Samuel Stein, *Capital City: Gentrification and the Real Estate State* (2019) and Daniel Stokols, *Social Ecology in the Digital Age: Solving Complex Problems in a Globalized World* (2018).

I also acknowledge with great gratitude the help provided me by staff at iUniverse including Reed Samuel, Jill Gaynor, Christine Colborne and Louie Angels.

Chapter 1

Introduction

At the time of this writing, people around the world see many important (and disturbing) trends providing a significant framework for trying to understand the future—not only for ourselves but especially for our children and grandchildren. The year 2018 saw important events providing a new and broader awareness of global warming and environmental devastation. Highly publicized reports by the United Nations, the United States government, and a major international conference in Katowice, Poland, coupled with significantly increased media attention, have placed the world's environmental problems as a significant focus of attention. Political discussion in 2019 in the United States has seen the promotion of "the Green New Deal." The years 2017 and 2018 also provided the experience of rising sea levels, increasing hurricanes, tornadoes, devastating forest fires, deadly tsunamis, increasing destruction of living creatures, and other planetary issues that are becoming more and more evident.

In this book, I will offer some concerns about how the most critically important of these trends interact and what are likely to be the difficult challenges that we and our future generations will be facing. Two fundamental causal trends to be highlighted are (1) the forecasted *global growth of urbanization* and (2) the *growing global power of the corporate world* and their key combined damaging roles in the Tragedy of the Commons. As an urban planner, I see these interlinked trends as a coming primary challenge for a very enlarged and difficult responsibility for urban planning.

In my title, I use the term *Tragedy of the Commons*. I feel the term well signifies what we are experiencing as we live through these critically important, destructive trends. A full clarification of this term is found in Wikipedia:

> The tragedy of the commons is a term used … to describe a situation in a shared-resource system where *individual users acting independently according to their own self-interest behave contrary to the common good of all users by depleting or spoiling that resource through their collective action.* The concept and phrase originated in an essay written in 1833 by the British economist William Forster Lloyd, who used a hypothetical example of the effects of unregulated grazing on common land (also known as a "common") in the British Isles. The concept became widely known over a century later due to an article written by the American ecologist and philosopher Garrett Hardin in 1968. In this modern economic context, <u>commons</u> is taken to mean any shared and unregulated resource such as atmosphere, oceans, rivers, fish stocks, or even an office refrigerator. (<u>https://en.wikipedia.org/wiki/Tragedy_of_the_commons</u>) (Emphasis added.) (G. Hardin, "The Tragedy of the Commons," *Science* 162, no. 3859 [1968]: 1243–48)

However, the tragedy we are currently facing is far broader and more complex than the original thinking around a small, common piece of farmland. Today, I argue, the commons is planet Earth, and many individual users—acting independently and according to their own self-interest—are behaving contrary to the common good of all users by endangering the planet through their private action.[1] Garrett Hardin warned that eventually humans must embrace *a world of limits*.

---

[1] Some readers might argue that with private property we don't have a commons as they had in early England. Yet whenever there is human interaction (especially economic), property lines are crossed, as are city and national boundaries. When a coal-powered plant delivers electricity to customers, air and water pollution occur along with GHG emissions, and property-owner lines are irrelevant. When a suburban driver leaves his or her privately owned property and drives a car to work, CO_2 emissions ignore all boundaries. Planet Earth is a commons.

Who Contributes to the Tragedy of the Commons?

In the broadest sense, who exactly is behind the Tragedy of the Commons? All of us. When heating our homes, what is the source of heat? What is the source of electricity in our homes? For almost everyone, the sources include coal, oil, and natural gas. For some people in the Global South, their housing may lack heating and cooling and electricity, and consequently, they are minor contributors. However, living in urban housing makes the clear majority of us contributors to the Tragedy of the Commons.

Driving an automobile also makes us contributors to the Tragedy of the Commons. Auto makers are involved in looking to electric cars and shared vehicles and expanded public transportation, but these are still focused on the future, and every person driving around a sprawling urban area today is a contributor to the Tragedy of the Commons.

Farmers in rural areas using fertilizers and insecticides help pollute waterways and thus contribute to the Tragedy of the Commons. Trucking companies moving freight over long distances add significantly to air pollution and greenhouse gas emissions and thus contribute to the Tragedy of the Commons.

The history of urban living since the Industrial Revolution in the nineteenth century has been one of global warming and the destruction of natural resources.

Accompanying that history has been the economy and the growing power of the global corporatist world. Clearly, the corporate use of coal, oil, and natural gas has been essential to the urbanization process, and these have contributed to the broad array of industrial production, financialization processes, and contemporary, new technologies.

A key contemporary trend is population growth and migration from rural to urban places (one of Garrett Hardin's original major concerns). This is explored more fully in Chapter 2.

A recent author, Ashley Dawson (2017), argues that the world's cities are the true primary cause of climate change and destruction of earth resources. This has been discussed by scientists for some time, with much literature pointing to the role of urbanization in environmental menacing since the nineteenth century. For me, the Tragedy of the Commons is primarily focused on urban areas expanding substantially in the next twenty-five to thirty years, which the United Nations has forecast. Given this, the question arises, what do we know of urban planning, and can this profession really help us in overcoming the urban Tragedy of the Commons of planet Earth? In the global world of professional education, urban planning is at best a small, limited profession. Its global roster is miniscule compared to the professions of law, medicine, and especially business.

Independent, broad, corporate economic action—powerfully dominant in today's global economy—is one of the key sources of damage to planet Earth. The basis for government institutions regulating independent economic action has become weaker and weaker. The regulated have taken control of the regulators. Government and other social institutions have become ruled by the global capitalist economy. As well, corporate economic activity primarily is focused on urban areas and is uncontrolled in determining the optimum land locations for corporate business activity and for premium housing for the wealthy or near wealthy.

How we all contribute to the Tragedy of the Commons has been well summarized by David Harvey:

> Nature has been modified by human action over the ages. The environment is a category that has to include the fields that have been cleared, the swamps and wetlands that have been drained, the rivers that have been re-engineered and the estuaries that have been dredged, the forests that have been cut over and re-planted, the roads, canals, irrigation systems, railroads, ports and harbours, airstrips and terminals that have been built, the dams, power-supply generators and electric grid systems that have been constructed, the water and sewer systems, cables and communications networks, vast cities, sprawling suburbs, factories, schools, houses, hospitals, shopping malls and tourist destinations galore. (Harvey 2010, 84)

Staff at the United Nations have informed us of current trends of people moving away from rural living to urban living, so that by 2050 two-thirds of the world's population will live in urban areas.[2] Economic trends may be confusing. Today, looking at the role of the corporatist activities, focusing not only on greed

---

[2] The European Commission has argued that urban population growth is already happening faster than the UN forecasts.

but also power, suggests both current and future difficulties. One of these prime difficulties is evident by the constantly growing level of inequality worldwide. This is the focus of Chapter 3. Economic power is also increasing control over governments and the diminishment of democratic governance, as explored in Chapter 4.

Additional notable trends are those in technological innovation (Chapter 5), from dominant communication technology to the use of robotics in industry, in the military, and in our homes. Consistently and historically, technological innovation has created circumstances that diminish the overall need for human labor. These are the key trends that I am looking at in the chapters that follow.

Have We Had Effective Urban Planning for the Tragedy of the Commons?

If urbanization is at the core of the Tragedy of the Commons, what is the importance of these new trends for those who are or might be involved, professionally or otherwise, in urban planning? We have had considerable literature in recent years discuss the successes and failures of urban planning in the twentieth century. This includes the criticism of the hardships entailed in the US in urban redevelopment work from the Housing Act of 1949, where active but "slum" neighborhoods were destroyed, replaced by high-rise, middle- and upper-income apartment towers or commercial/industrial parks.

A deeper criticism has emerged from the phenomena of urban sprawl, inspired by the concepts of English "garden cities"; by the nineteenth-century development of "streetcar suburbs" (Warner 1978); by Frederick law Olmstead's Riverside, Illinois; and by Frank Lloyd Wright's "Broadacre City." Sprawl was also stimulated by the massive ownership of automobiles in the twentieth century, combined with the rapid, intensified preference for owning a single-family home on a private, single lot of land. In the United States, this was also fortified by the Federal Housing Administration in the time just after World War II (unfortunately, an FHA official encouragement at that time included promoting racial segregation). Finally, the US Interstate Highway program facilitated urban sprawl in significant ways. Urban sprawl has been dominant in the United States since the 1950s, but I also observed signs abroad of suburban sprawl as I was working in Central and

Eastern Europe in the 1990s, when those nations were overcoming communist rule and seeking to move to free market democracies.

Low-density urban development has created many difficulties for contemporary urban areas, beginning with high levels of traffic congestion, significant environmental pollution and damage, and loss of farmland and woodland. Today, we have also become more aware of significant, negative psychological and health impacts of sprawl living.

An overall criticism of the work of the urban planning profession has been offered by Samuel Stein (2019). He was educated in urban planning but early in his book he argues:

> "By the end of my education, I realized that capitalism makes the best of planning impossible: any good that planners do is filtered through a system that dispossesses those who cannot pay." (Stein, 2019, 9)

An excellent summary of the relation of urban planning and capitalism is also provided by Michael Dear:

> "Urban planning is always situated within the framework of existing relations of authority and subordination in capitalist society, and these relations regulate its identity and function." (Dear, 1981, iv.)

Perhaps the most important trend is that discussed for the past sixty years or so—climate change or global warming. This trend has entailed significant scientific exploration on an ongoing basis since Rachel Carson's book, *The Silent Spring*, published in 1962. Continued concern was enhanced by the book by Donna Meadows et al., *The Limits to Growth*, published in 1972.

The United Nations has played a leading role in drawing attention to climate change and environmental destruction. There have been many international conferences hosted by the United Nations since the 1960s.

In the United States, President Jimmy Carter was an early advocate of environmental concerns, as noted in his report *Global 2000*.[3] The year 1972 was also the occasion for the United Nations conference on the human environment, held in Stockholm, Sweden. In 1983, the UN set up the World Commission on the Environment and Development (WCED), which then produced the *Brundtland Report*, published in 1987, that focused on sustainability. This led to the 1987 Montréal protocol that was successful in stopping the depletion of the ozone layer. This was followed by the 1992 international conference that took place in Rio de Janeiro. The Kyoto Protocol took place in Japan in 1997 and involved great debate as to procedures for reducing carbon emissions. In 2001, the United States abandoned the Kyoto Protocol. In 2002, the World Summit on Sustainable Development was held in Johannesburg. This meeting was also highlighted by obstructionism by the United States.[4]

In December 2015, the Paris Agreement was forged, an agreement within the United Nations Framework Convention on Climate Change (UNFCCC), dealing with greenhouse gas emissions mitigation, adaptation, and finance, starting in the year 2020. Representatives of 196 state parties negotiated the agreement. In October 2018, the UNIPCC report was issued, arguing that global warming is occurring faster than in the past, and in November 2018, the US National Climate Assessment Report was issued. In December 2018, the COP24 International Conference was in Katowice, Poland, with further agreed-upon international policy rules for environmental action.

Over time, these discussion efforts have become very political. We have recently seen the election of a United States president who believes climate change is a hoax and who appointed a director of the US Environmental Protection Agency who firmly agreed and took up relaxation of regulations in coal, oil, natural gas, and chemical manufacturing. He stepped down due to personal corruption, but his replacement has

---

[3] After Jimmy Carter, Ronald Reagan was elected president. Reagan took the exact opposite view when he made the claim "trees cause more pollution than automobiles do." Today, US president Donald Trump has proclaimed that climate change is a "hoax" and has followed policies to dismantle environmental science and policy.

[4] For an excellent discussion on the history of efforts at reaching agreements on climate change, see Simon Dresner, *The Principles of Sustainability*, Second Edition (London: Earthscan, 2008). This book is also an excellent philosophical analysis of the concept of sustainability.

been equally committed to coal and coal power. Scientists have also been dropped from the Environmental Protection Agency payroll. Irrespective of contemporary political debate, however, there is clearly strong evidence of significant climate change that is important as our most primary key trend as we face the future.

In this global setting, the fundamental trend is that of the global population coming to live more and more in urban areas. In 1980, about 35 percent of the global population lived in urban areas. In 1990, the global urban population had grown to 39 percent. Then, half of the world's population lived in urban areas by 2004. The expectation today is that two-thirds of the world's population will live in urban areas by 2050.

Urban population forecasts have far-reaching implications. New urban growth will likely greatly expand the challenges spelled out above.

The second key trend has been the movement away from free market economics toward very strong, corporate, near-monopoly economic dominance. This dominance is leading toward not only control of major human consumer needs but also control over sovereign nation states. This dominance is evident by the increasing creation of oligopolies. There are many of these clusters of corporations that on the surface appear to be competitors. However, they are interlinked and colluding entities exercising control over needed commodities such as food, energy, and medicine. Control also means eliminating competition—contrary to the fundamentals of free market economics. Corporate oligopoly control is also dominating national and subnational governments through persistent effort to minimize regulation and lawful operations as well as growing dominance in international military armaments. Today's economic dominance is the clear arena where individual users acting independently, according to their own self-interest, behave contrary to the common good of all users by depleting or spoiling resources through their collective action.

The change from a free market economy in the United States and in other countries to a global corporatist economy has been going on for some time. Today, my best chances for opening a new business will occur in very different circumstances. If I were a chef and wanted to open a restaurant, I would have the usual tasks of securing funds, acquiring a good location, installing equipment, and hiring staff. At some point in the process, I would find major corporate control of food products. For most standard products (dairy products, salad dressing, sugar, salt, coffee, and even beer and chicken), I would encounter products that are produced by oligopoly ownership. I could rely on local food production for fresh foods (at least in warm-weather seasons). Even here, however, a few large corporations control the production and sale of agricultural seeds, fertilizers, insecticides, and so forth. Moreover, if I were to try to open a local neighborhood pharmacy here in the United States, I would quickly run into the dynamics of the corporatist economy and would soon feel pressure from the corporate powers of CVS, Walgreens, or Walmart.

Another trend is growing innovative technology. Robotic development has influenced manufacturing production for some time. In addition, we have already experienced extensively the worldwide technology of artificial intelligence and social communication. We are now seeing the slow but active move toward driverless and electrical cars and buses, along with driverless, independent aircraft drones. Additionally, commodity delivery is changing the nature of retailing. Innovation and creativity in medicine and health care have long been supported, yet pharmaceutical development and production has become a major oligopoly, resulting in significant unrestricted increases in the pricing of medical prescriptions.

Of major importance has been the role of information technology and artificial intelligence. This technology has been instrumental in creating economic networks that have significantly lowered the costs of global corporate mergers and acquisitions and has aided corporate interlocking and collusion, and even illegal tax avoidance, money laundering, and hiding. Information technology has altered the character of labor force demand with more and more occupational characteristics being dependent on higher-level education in digitizing skills. Information technology has also had social and political implications that have been exposed by the role of the Facebook Corporation in fostering fake news and information.[5] The role of artificial technology in attacking personal privacy has become a serious global problem.

The combination of these trends produces serious questions about the nature of human life in the coming decades of the twenty-first century throughout the planet—especially in urban areas. Thus, the goal of this book is to explore the nature of these critical global trends and tackle the emerging questions. How should we engage in planning to prevent and overcome these highly destructive trends?

The book is organized in the following fashion.

---

[5] The Facebook role in the US presidential election of 2016, along with its global role in influencing false or highly controversial social information, was well portrayed by a PBS two-part *Frontline* program shown on October 29 and October 30, 2018.

Chapter 2 focuses on the forecasts of population recently set forth by the United Nations Department of Economic and Social Affairs, Population Division. These forecasts are globally presented by countries and specific urban areas. Today, for example, there are twenty-eight urban areas around the world comprising megacities of more than ten million people. Between now and 2030, the UN is forecasting another twelve will grow beyond the ten million population. In short, in just a decade, it will be a world of forty megacities. China and India are predicted to see the major growth in megacities.

The UN has also forecast 2030 populations for all urban areas that currently have at least three hundred thousand people. This chapter also discusses a few questions that need to be raised about forecast accuracy, particularly issues such as the availability of potable water and the limitations of planetary resources. Also noted is the dominance of coastal location for the larger urban areas.

Chapter 3 takes up the trends of corporate dominance over the world economy, trends that started in the 1970s and grew in momentum in the 1980s. The chapter is focused on the nature of oligopolies that dominate the world's economic, social, and political life. There is significant literature today on this domination, and the chapter will highlight some of the major points from many writings. I have also examined available data concerning illegal or unethical practices that seem to be widespread in these oligopolies. The chapter also discusses how they affect general economic relations in urban areas. There is considerable research reviewed regarding United States and European urban areas. Investigation of economic growth in China and India is also explored.

Chapter 4 explores the relationship of global corporatism and global governance. Most of this impact is examined in the United States, where the relationships of major world corporations and US national and state governments have frequently been in one-sided agreement. Corporate finances and political pressures often provide strong dominance over the governance process. Journalism in the USA has placed great stress on corporate or billionaire financial contributions to American elections. There is also even greater financial investment in daily interaction with the United States Congress through the lobbying process. In the United States, the Roberts Supreme Court has provided major legal decisions abetting the use of corporate wealth to take control and diminish economic regulation. This leads to the question of the future of democratic societies. Evidence suggests that the democracies of the developed world are showing signs of institutional decline. This is accompanied by the global rise of the Chinese economy, an economy under the political control of an authoritative dictator government.

Chapter 5 discusses the many technological trends that are current and active around the world. Most important is the digital artificial intelligence technology that has provided instantaneous communication in a global economy, allowing for formation of oligopoly networks at virtually little cost. We have changed business transactions, including the digital exchange of money that diminishes paper bills and metal coins on an international scale. Artificial intelligence has vastly expanded the field of political discourse internationally. It is significantly altering the nature of retail business. As one writer argues, this has made the world of corporate dominance and collusion easier and cheaper to follow (Sassen 2012). Recent research has also shown that digital technology has fashioned significant negative impacts for the global labor force.

Of major import has been technological changes in energy. The environmental consequences of earlier machineries involving oil, coal, and natural gas are addressed today with increasing reliance on solar, wind, and hydroelectric technologies. The United States, however, given the economic dominance of the oil industry and current United States policies, tends to emphasize a continued importance of petroleum, natural gas, and coal, including expanded offshore drilling.

Creative technology has already had major effects on manufacturing processes. The use of robots in the manufacturing of industrial products has been increasing for many years. Emerging technology changes in transportation are being forecast to considerably alter patterns of accessibility in urban areas. These include driverless electric cars and drone aircraft. The driverless drone aircraft first had extensive use in war but now approaches plans for civilian business use (in fact, drones provide exceptional 3-D photography in urban areas).

The importance of farming and technology is also discussed in chapter 5. Food for the future urban population is very important. The agricultural industry has, in the past, been guilty of serious environmental problems in aquifer depletion and sending fertilizers and other pollutants into water resources. Chapter 5 provides a list of current and likely future farming innovations—some that are positive and helpful and some that are very negative.

Chapter 6 takes up the role of the coming urban land-development process, given the UN forecasts shown in chapter 2. With worldwide urban growth, the question of how the emerging planetary urban land space will accommodate population growth is critical, given the increasing dominance of the corporate world in the acquisition, control, and development of land—in short, corporate real estate. Very important in urban development is the construction and financing of housing (generally at costs aimed at upper-income customers). During the twentieth century, in the world's developed countries, local contractors, realtors, and banks predominantly carried this out for middle- and upper-class families. The twentieth century did see strong efforts at public housing in many countries after World War II.[6] Public housing, however, has greatly declined in the twenty-first century.

In the twenty-first century, there is increasing consolidation of these activities into larger and larger corporate entities in geographically dispersed urban areas. Corporate interests have long dominated the development of offices, factories, and retail spaces. Office buildings have dominated central business districts, but after World War II, they often also developed suburban clusters. Today, in retailing, we have the corporate dominance of Walmart and Target and their big-box, predominantly suburban retail outlets, plus the strong mail order trend of one the world's largest corporations, Amazon.

Chapter 7 is my call for an expansion of urban planning education toward achieving sustainable planetary goals. Training for urban planners must go far beyond architecture and urban design and push creators to broader *transdisciplinary* skills.[7] Fundamental to the issues these trends offer is the question of local government power. The historic tendency is that local governments are typically overseen by national sovereignty and power. Yet, with the above trends, this has been changing in an increasingly

---

[6] In the nineteenth century, in the United States' western territories, housing was often developed with neighbors pooling individual resources, labor, and material to construct housing. In the twentieth century, this often happened in the undeveloped world. People built their own housing without the benefit of any regulation concerning zoning, building codes, plumbing, or sanitation. Much of the housing development in Africa and Asia has taken place in this fashion.

[7] A good example of this is at Arizona State University, which has established a School for Sustainability that includes the urban planning program that was moved from the School of Architecture. Another is the School of Social Ecology at the University of California, Irvine, that also includes their urban planning program.

economic, corporate command. The dominance of corporate interests in the land-development process suggests even greater challenges for urban planning in the institutional settings of global local governments.

Given the trends outlined in the previous chapters, Chapter 8 is an epilogue exploring the nature of dealing with future urban growth in a dominant corporatist economy and how it will differ from the practices and experience of the twentieth century in urban development. The chapter is generalist in nature, talking about how corporate leaders, philanthropists, journalists, and educational leaders should increase their responsibilities toward ending the planet Earth's Tragedy of the Commons.

All these trends are identified with considerable literature by scholars from many different disciplines and journalists. Putting them all together raises significant questions about the nature of creating the living conditions for our children and grandchildren. With my background in urban planning, there are clearly serious questions about how we might plan for these trends in order that their urban consequences can be influenced by more sophisticated and effective public and private policies. Thus, problems the world over need to be given far more widespread discussion and concern as *sustainability problems occurring primarily in global urban areas*. We need greatly expanded attention from not only government officials but also socially responsible corporate leaders, philanthropic leaders, NGO leaders, academic leaders, journalists, and international citizenry.

The United Nations has set forth a series of seventeen sustainable development goals. The following summarizes those goals laid out for the year 2030:

People

We are determined to end poverty and hunger, in all their forms and dimensions, and to ensure that all human beings can fulfil their potential in dignity and equality and in a healthy environment.

Planet

We are determined to protect the planet from degradation, including through sustainable consumption and production, sustainably managing its natural resources and taking urgent action on climate change, so that it can support the needs of the present and future generations.

Prosperity

We are determined to ensure that all human beings can enjoy prosperous and fulfilling lives and that *economic, social and technological progress occurs in harmony with nature.* (Emphasis added.) (https://sustainabledevelopment.un.org/post2015/transformingourworld)

In many respects, the following chapters raise significant questions as to whether these goals are achievable. Economic, social, and political trends show growing poverty and inequality and increasing planetary ruin. These UN goals seem to require us to change our current behavioral trends by 180 degrees.

Thus, the book addresses this question: are we facing public-private partnership or public-private warfare or overall human decline? How can we train future young people with education, foresight, and normative values to meaningfully tackle these challenges and provide better living for everyone in this radically changing world? How might we best learn of how we may overcome and stop the Tragedy of the Commons impacting planet Earth?

References

Carson, R. 1962. *The Silent Spring.* New York: Houghton Mifflin Company.

Dawson, A. 2017. *Extreme Cities: The Peril and Promise of Urban Life in the Age of Climate Change.* London–New York: Verso.

Dear, M. and A.J. Scott, Editors 1981. *Urbanization and Urban Planning in Capitalist Society.* New York and Oxon, UK: Routledge.

Department of Economic and Social Affairs, United Nations. 2015. *World Urbanization Prospects: the 2014 Revision.* United Nations: New York.

Dresner, S. 2008. *The Principles of Sustainability.* 2nd ed. London: Earthscan.

Hardin, G. 1968. "The Tragedy of the Commons." *Science* 162 (3859): 1243–48.

Harvey, D. 2010. *The Enigma of Capital and the Crisis of Capitalism.* New York: Oxford University Press.

Meadows, D. H., D. L. Meadows, J. Randers, and W. W. Behrens III. 1972. *The Limits to Growth.* New York: Universe Books.

Melillo, Jerry M., Terese (T. C.) Richmond, and Gary W. Yohe, eds. 2014. *Climate Change Impacts in the United States: The Third National Climate Assessment.* US Global Change Research Program, 841. doi:10.7930/J0Z31WJ2.

Sassen, S. 2012. *Cities in a World Economy.* 4th ed. Los Angeles: Pine Forge Press (Sage).

Stein, S. 2019. *Capital City: Gentrification and the Real Estate State.* London, New York: Verso Books.

"Transforming Our World: The 2030 Agenda for Sustainable Development." https://sustainabledevelopment.un.org/post2015/transformingourworld.

Warner, S. B., Jr. 1978. *Streetcar Suburbs: The Process of Growth in Boston, 1870–1900.* 2nd ed. Cambridge, MA: Harvard University Press.

Websites:

https://cop24.gov.pl/.

Chapter 2

Urban Population Growth

With all the progress of urban development since World War II, there have been silent trends that can be associated with planet Earth's Tragedy of the Commons.

Thus, a central challenge in the coming decades comes from the global projections for increased urban growth found in the extensive reports from the United Nations Department of Economic and Social Affairs, Population Division. Their studies were the foundation for the Habitat III conference in Quito, Ecuador, in 2016. These studies highlight the increasing difficulty in world urban planning.

The following is from their 2014 report, *World Urbanization Prospects: The 2014 Revision*:

> Globally, more people live in urban areas than rural areas, 54% of the world's population residing in urban areas in 2014. In 1950, 30% of the world's population was urban, and by 2050, 66% of the world's population is projected to be urban. There is significant diversity in the urbanization levels reached by different regions. The most urbanized regions include North America (82% living in urban areas in 2014), Latin America and the Caribbean (80%), and Europe (73%). In contrast, Africa and Asia remained mostly rural, with only 40% of their respective populations living in urban areas. All regions are expected to urbanize further over the coming

decades. Africa and Asia are urbanizing faster than the other regions and are projected to become 56 and 64% urban, respectively, by 2050.

In short, the report argues that 90 percent of the urban population increase between 2014 and 2030 will be in Asia and Africa. There is already substantial evidence that growth is occurring very strongly and China and India. Cities in already developed countries (USA and Europe) are expected to add only 130 million people to their populations during this period. Cities in less developed countries are expected to grow by 2.3 billion people (United Nations Population Division 2014, files 2 and 3).

The 2014 report methodology is primarily demographic. It includes the study of mortality, fertility, and international and internal migration, including their levels and trends as well as their causes and consequences. The report makes estimates and projections of population size, age and sex structure, and demographic indicators for all countries of the world. The report also examines the relationship between socioeconomic development and population change as well as the documentation analysis of population-development policies at the national and international levels. The overall trend lincs for world urban and rural populations can be seen in figure 2.1.

The UN report deals with growth of all urban areas with three hundred thousand people or more in all regions and countries in the world from 1950 to 2014, with projections to 2030. The report thus provides population estimates and projections for 1,692 urban settlements. This broad global increase in urban population poses serious problems with respect to their geographic land planning. A critical problem, of course, is the history of urban development and its contribution to contemporary problems of global warming, health-endangering pollution, and destruction of planetary resources. An additional aspect of these challenges lies in the fact that much of this growth will be fostering the rapid (and unplanned?) expansion of megacities (cities of more than ten million people).[8]

---

[8] Recent work by the European Commission raises questions about the United Nations' forecasts. They suggest the UN forecasts are very conservative and that the world urban population has already reached levels that are higher than the UN forecasts. The Commission, along with other researchers, raised questions about how an urban area is defined. They point to inconsistencies in national methods of defining urban areas and determining existing populations. The European Commission, along with the New York University Expansion Project, used methods involving satellite imagery, GIS, and advanced statistical analysis. http://www.thisisplace.org/i/?id=0150beca-e3f5-47e0-bc74-9ccc5ef1db8a.

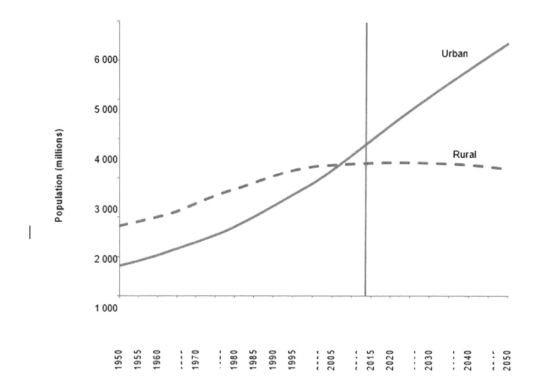

Figure 2.1. Past and future global, urban, and rural population

United Nations Department of Economic and Social Affairs/Population Division. World Urbanization Prospects: the 2014 Revision. Figure I.i, p. 7

The Emergence of Megacities

Major urban growth is already underway. As the UN report notes, there are currently twenty-eight urban regions whose population exceeds ten million people. The report also notes only ten such large urban regions existed in 1990; thus, the world has seen growth of eighteen new huge urban complexes in the past twenty-four years. It is quite clear, therefore, the world population is predominantly moving toward already large urban centers. Table 2.1 shows the twenty-eight urban areas that exceeded ten million people in 2014. Table 2.2 shows the twelve urban areas that the UN predicts will be added to today's twenty-eight by 2030.

Table 2.1. Twenty-eight cities with a population of at least ten million people in 2014

• Tokyo, Japan	37.8 Million		• Istanbul, Turkey	14.0 M
• Delhi, India	24.9 M		• Chongqing, China	12.9 M
• Shanghai, China	23.0 M		• Rio de Janeiro, Brazil	12.8 M
• Mexico City, Mexico	20.8 M		• Manila, Philippines	12.8 M
• Sao Paulo, Brazil	20.8 M		• Lagos, Nigeria	12.6 M
• Mumbai (Bombay), India	20.7 M		• Los Angeles, USA	12.3 M
• Osaka, Japan	20.1 M		• Moscow, Russia	12.0 M
• Beijing, China	19.5 M		• Guangzhou, Guangdong, China	11.8 M
• New York, USA	18.6 M		• Kinshasa, Dem. Rep. of Congo	11.1 M
• Cairo, Egypt	18.4 M		• Tianjin, China	10.9 M
• Dhaka, Bangladesh	17.0 M		• Paris, France	10.8 M
• Karachi, Pakistan	16.1 M		• Shenzhen, China	10.7 M
• Buenos Aires, Argentina	15.0 M		• London, United Kingdom	10.2 M
• Calcutta, India	14.8 M		• Jakarta, Indonesia	10.2 M

From: Department of Economic and Social Affairs, United Nations (2015). *World Urbanization Prospects.* 2014 revision. United Nations: New York, table 2, page 26.

Table 2.2. The forecasted 2030 population of ten new cities with more than ten million people

• Bangalore, India	14.8 Million		• Johannesburg, South Africa	11.5 M
• Madras, India	13.9 M		• Bangkok, Thailand	11.5 M
• Lahore, Pakistan	13.0 M		• Ahmadabad, India	10.5 M
• Hyderabad, India	12.8 M		• Luanda, Angola	10.4 M
• Lima, Peru	12.2 M		• Ho Chi Minh, Vietnam	10.2 M
• Bogota, Colombia	11.9 M		• Chengdu, China	10.1 M

From: Department of Economic and Social Affairs, United Nations. 2015. *World Urbanization Prospects.* 2014 revision. United Nations: New York, table 2, pages 26, 27.

Today, the megacities are concentrated in Asia and Latin America. Six are in China, three are in India, two are in Japan, and two are in Brazil. In the United States, it's only New York and Los Angeles. Other megacities in the developed world of course are Moscow, Paris, and London. Tokyo is clearly the largest megacity in the world, but it also suggests there may be demographic determinants of some decline for this area in the next ten to fifteen years. Table 2.1 shows that urban areas this large tend not to be in the developed world. Immigration to urban areas tends to concentrate on already large urban centers.

> In a major development, the Chinese government last year showcased its renewed war on poverty by announcing an ambitious strategy to transfer much of China's population from rural to urban areas. The hope is the approach will lead to higher standards of living for China's rural poor and heightened domestic consumer demand. Earlier restrictions on internal migration had created a de-facto illegal migrant population in many Chinese cities, without access to government services. This had been cited as a source of social instability and served to highlight the uneven distribution of benefits from China's economic growth. Chinese leaders must ensure adequate food supplies for a surging urban population while simultaneously promoting rural depopulation – a difficult juggling act in view of an oft expressed goal of ensuring national self- sufficiency in food production. (Barry Mirkin, Yale Global)

The best way to get a sense of the distribution of these megacities around the globe is to view a map showing the basic locations. Figure 2.2 shows the map of the world with the locations of all the cities with more than three hundred thousand people, as studied by the UN. This first map shows the location of all urban areas of three hundred thousand in three different times: 1990, 2014, and then projected to 2030.

There are key things to note on this first map. Given the climate change phenomena we are currently experiencing, it is important to note that many urban areas are in coastal regions. The exceptions to this are in the Midwest of the United States and on the European continent. China and India have extensive interior cities as well. Yet the coastal areas are predominant locations of urban centers on virtually every continent.

This is also true of the megacities with populations greater than ten million, as well as of the UN's projected megacities for 2030.

Figure 2.2. Map of world cities by size: 1990, 2014, and 2030

From: United Nations Department of Economic and Social Affairs. *World Urbanization Prospects.* 2014 revision. Figure I.12, page 19.

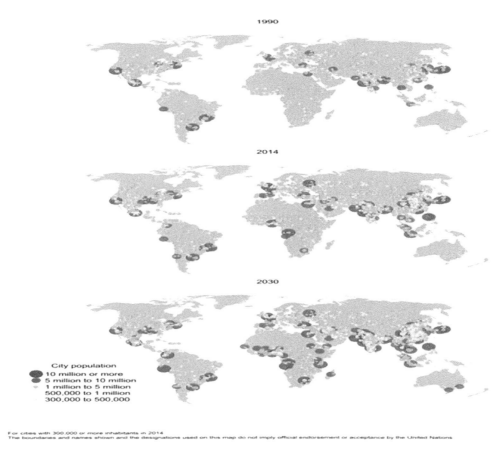

It is important to focus on megacities since these are urban developments for which there is extremely little experience in traditional urban planning. Effective, ongoing control of land use, density, housing, and infrastructure (water supply, waste management, transportation) is mostly problematic in virtually all megacities, creating many serious and highly expensive problems for residents and for local governments attempting to manage development. This has been especially true in the global regions where urban growth has been most rapid. These areas are shown on the maps that follow.

Figures 2.3 and 2.4 portray global maps with urban growth dimensions. Figure 2.3 shows the growth rates between 1990 and 2018 of all urban centers (population of more than three hundred thousand), ranging from cities with lower rates of growth (less than 1 percent) to cities with relatively high rates of growth (more than 5 percent). Figure 2.3 is distinctive in that high growth rates between 1990 and 2018 have already focused on coastal regions. Exceptionally high growth was also seen in China and India, not only in coastal areas but also interiors. West Africa also showed high rates of growth in the past fourteen years.

Figure 2.4 portrays United Nations projections for city growth forward to 2030. This generally suggests that individual growth rates will generally be less than 5 percent. In addition, distinctive in figure 2.4 is that most cities in developed countries will be slowly growing at rates less than 1 percent. This slow growth rate is also the case for most of the megacities in the world. Perhaps the most important feature from figure 2.4 is the continuing concentration of small and modest-sized urban areas in coastal regions.

Figure 2.3. Urban growth 1990–2018

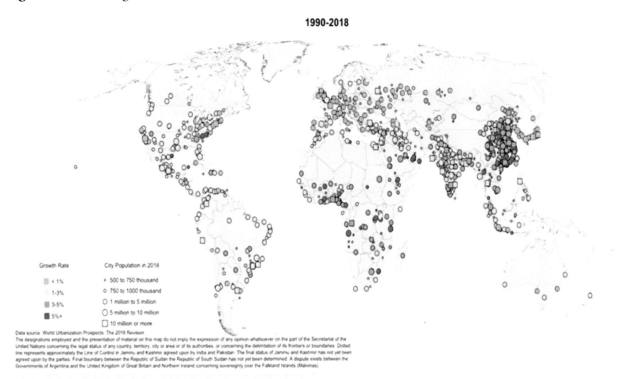

Map from United Nations at: https://population.un.org/wup/Maps/.

Figure 2.4. Urban growth 2018–2030

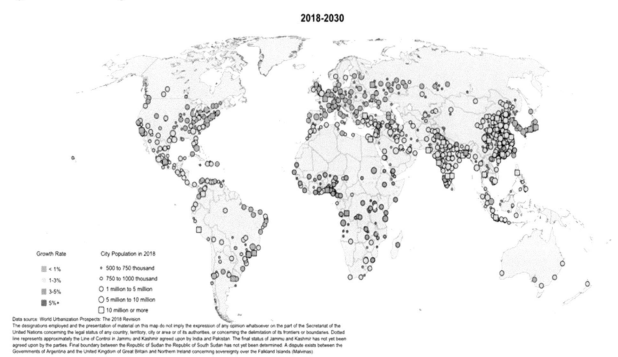

Map from United Nations at: <u>https://population.un.org/wup/Maps/.</u>

UN Sustainability Goals

The United Nations has also set out seventeen sustainable development goals. These are shown in box 2.1.

Box 2.1. United Nations seventeen sustainable development goals

1. No poverty

2. Zero hunger

3. Good health and well-being

4. Quality education

5. Gender equality

6. Clean water and sanitation

7. Affordable and clean energy

8. Decent work and economic growth

9. Industry innovation and infrastructure

10. Reduced inequalities

11. Sustainable cities and communities

12. Responsible consumption and production

13. Climate action

14. Life below water

15. Life on land

16. Peace, justice, and strong institutions

17. Partnerships for the goals

In the chapters that follow will be analyses as to the likelihood of these goals being achieved by 2030, 2050, or even 2100. The rise of urban populations will also be accompanied by an economic system trending toward greater and greater inequality. The economic system is also exhibiting significant control over governments and threatening weakening democracy. We can also see growing innovation and creativity bringing technological development of various sorts. These show positive direction, but they also show negative effects, the most important of which will be technological machinery substituting for human labor. It is also evident that the controlling economic system has little acknowledgment of climate action and environmental harm. The chapters that follow will suggest that it will take major changes in the contemporary global economics and governance if we are truly going to eliminate poverty and inequality and thrive on the UN sustainability goals. For the chapters that follow, goal 11, sustainable cities and communities, is the goal overarching all the others, given the direction of urban population growth.

Limits to Urban Growth? Questions Regarding Forecasts

When I graduated with my city planning degree, I was confident that I would never have trouble predicting the future. We were taught all kinds of quantitative and qualitative methods, particularly with the availability of mathematic and statistical modeling techniques and strong empirical trend lines. After a few years of professional practice, I began to have doubts, leading me to read the work of Karl Popper, a leading physicist and philosopher. He raised profound questions about our ability to forecast the future, particularly regarding human interaction (Popper 1945, *The Open Society and Its Enemies*).

Numerous analyses, particularly of the social sciences, raise serious questions about our ability to see the future (Bolan 2017). One author suggested that it was not possible to predict beyond a five-year future (Banfield, E. 1970). There are many reasons behind this, but clearly, the large-scale trend lines of global population growth are nevertheless consistent and constant. Circumstances do provide some questioning of this dominance of urban growth relative to rural and total growth in the coming years. There is discussion in the contemporary political world about the possibilities of nuclear warfare, which would clearly interfere with the realization of these population forecasts. There is also some question about the role of global climate change and how that may influence future urban growth, particularly in coastal regions. For the United States alone, the year 2017 saw record-breaking hurricane destruction in Houston, Florida, Puerto Rico, and Caribbean islands. It was also a year of significant forest fires in the United States, especially in California. Significant earthquakes in Mexico and Iraq added to the full traumatic episodes of the year 2017. The next year, 2018, saw two new hurricanes in the US, along with more major fires in California and a major tsunami and earthquake in Indonesia.

Amidst these urban population forecasts, it is important to keep in mind crucial global environmental factors in the urbanization process. A recent APA report states the situation quite clearly:

> Water is essential for human life. It is necessary to support human settlement and the built environment. Water is crucial for ecosystem functioning and the production of food and energy. Water provides important economic and aesthetic values for cities, counties, and towns. From the beginning of civilization, human beings have devised ways to ensure that water is available when and where it is needed, as well as ways of addressing wastewater and of dealing with storms and flooding. (Cesanek, W., V. Elmer, and J. Graeff. 2017. *Planners and Water*. PAS Report 588. American Planning Association. Page 15.)

Figure 2.5 provides a global map showing water stress indicators. This generally indicates the areas of the globe that have availability of water ranging from fully adequate to seriously inadequate. Here we see regions of the world where inadequacy of water supplies may seriously hamper urban growth. The most dominant region is clearly the Middle East. I have always felt that once Middle Easterners decide to stop their religious wars, they will then go to war over water. Another key area is in the Midwest Central, USA, where a long history of heavy farming has meant a key depletion of a very important, large, and extensive aquifer. California has long had problems with water supply. Areas of Texas and Mexico also show difficulties with water supply. The Sahara Desert has always been known as an area deplete of water, but North Africa and sub-Saharan Africa and Eastern Australia are also facing critical water problems.

As Daniel Stokols points out:

> Many of the world's largest urban centers are located along shorelines or on estuaries. Nearly 45% of the world's population lives within 150 km (100 miles) of a coast, and upward of 200 million people now residing near shorelines face significant flooding risks and eventual forced migration from sea level rise by the end of the century. (Stokols 2018, 237)

A major omission in the United Nations population report is the question of climate change and how well we and future generations will be able to manage and control the increases in world temperature and their impact on coastal urbanity and urban heat islands generally. From the United Nations report, I have prepared estimates of future populations in urban coastal regions, living in urban areas having more than five million people today. These are shown in table 2.3. These very large urban areas will clearly face difficulties arising from growing, warming, and acidic sea levels.[9]

---

[9] Two new books have recently published on this problem: (1) *Extreme Cities* by Andrew Dawson (2017) and (2) *The Water Will Come* by Jeff Goodell (2017). Full details in references to this chapter.

Figure 2.5. Global availability of water

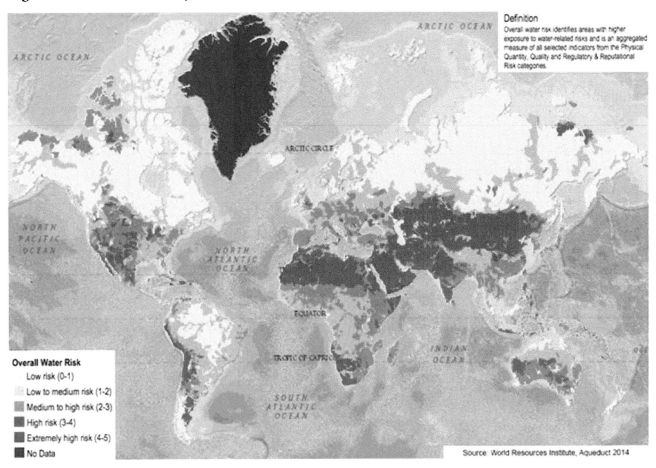

World Resources Institute

Table 2.3. Prospects for population growth in urban coastal regions

	Number of urban areas over 5 million	2014 population in millions	2030 population in millions
Urban area with population over 5 million	71	753.4	962.7
Coastal urban areas with population over 5 million	36	434.6	539.7
Coastal percent of all over 5 million population urban areas	50.1%	57.7%	56.1%
Average population of all 71 (2014) urban areas over 5 million		10.1	13.6
Average population of all 36 (2014) coastal urban areas over 5 million		12.2	15.0

Among the people focused on climate and environmental issues, there has been a rise in what has been called Neo-Malthusian theory. Global environmental concerns extend beyond the questions of oceans rising and temperature increasing. The emission of carbon dioxide has additional effects that may have serious implications for urban life. Analyses show that not only do oceans rise, but they are also becoming warmer and more acidic. Life on ocean coral reefs has demonstrated decline and death. Some chemical emissions (such as chlorofluorocarbon [CFC]) diminished the ozone layer that surrounds the planet and protects us from direct sunlight. Without the ozone layer, there would be no living creatures on the planet—human or otherwise.[10] Also affected are important nitrogen levels and phosphorus levels. An excellent summary of the climate and earth-resource problems facing the planet is found in the early chapters of a Nobel-winning book by William Nordhaus, *The Climate Casino: Risk, Uncertainty, and Economics for a Warming World* (2013, Part I).

Another effect of human activity—particularly economic activity—has been the loss of biodiversity. Some years ago, economist Herman Daly wrote an excellent book arguing that we should not be promoting

---

[10] Fortunately, steps were taken in the 1980s to severely limit the destruction of the ozone layer by limiting CFC emissions.

economic growth but rather environmental stability. Science, with these concerns, argues that the resources of the earth are not infinite. Given the extent of projected urbanization and economic activity, it is appropriate to do more to limit global warming.

In short, urbanization has substantially increased global environmental damage. As urban population grows over the next twenty to thirty years, the prospects of achieving the UN's sustainable development goals pose significant scientific, economic, social, and political challenges. Figure 2.6 provides a diagrammatic outline of the principal concerns of the Neo-Malthusian theory, pointing out a fuller range of climate change dynamics.

Finally, with cities forecasted to grow so rapidly and to such a large extent, exactly how livable will they be? A recent study by Brazilian Robert Muggah, published on the CityLab website, suggests that much of this urban growth may be very fragile. He described his research method as follows:

> In order to empirically measure urban fragility, I broadened the lens to eleven risk factors, including the speed of population growth, levels of unemployment, income inequality, access to basic services (electricity), homicide rates, terrorism, conflict events, and exposure to natural hazards (including cyclones, droughts, and floods). My research extends to over 2,100 cities with populations of at least 250,000 inhabitants over a 15-year period. (Muggah, 2017,2)

He goes on to describe his major findings of international urban growth of the past fifteen years:

> One of the dominant drivers of fragility appears to be rapid unregulated urbanization. When cities grow fast—over 3 percent a year—city fragility is more likely. This is because cities experiencing sprawling slums, such as Karachi and Kinshasa, are also more predisposed to physical dispersion and social disorganization. Those are in turn correlated with crime and violence. (Ibid.,2)

By contrast, cities registering lower population growth rates tend to be more stable. As Robert Muggah notes:

> Other drivers of urban fragility related to concentrated disadvantage, include inequality, unemployment, and poverty. From Baltimore to Lagos, criminal violence tends to be more prolific in unequal cities compared to those with a more equal distribution of income and basic services. Real and relative deprivation of income, property, service provision and social status are all connected to reduced social capital and social efficacy. (Ibid,., 2)

In addition, rapid immigration into growing urban areas may precede economic development in those areas, leaving a city with a significant surplus of laborers and few prospects for employment and wages. In short, while the trend lines certainly suggest the growth of the worldwide urban population, it is not clear what sort of living conditions will be realized in 2030 and 2050. It most pointedly raises questions. Given the inequality throughout the world, as will be described in the next chapter, accompanied by lack of basic social services and high crime rates, will the cities of 2030 and 2050 be more livable than today or will they be significantly less livable?

Implications for the Role of the Urban Planning Profession

If the forecasts of the United Nations are accurate, there are significant new challenges for the urban planning process, along with the challenges presented in the following chapters. One analyst, Shlomo Angel, stated:

> Worse yet, researchers ... often chose to study cities in more developed countries and then offer urban policy recipes for cities in less developed ones, where conditions— rapid rates of population growth, inadequate municipal or housing finance, and weak rule of law, for example—make the transfer of knowledge, policy prescriptions, and planning practices rather irrelevant. (Shlomo Angel 2016, *Atlas of Urban Expansion*, xviii)

These planning challenges are summarized here and will be taken up in more detail in chapters 6 and 7. They broadly include the following:

- dealing with city size, land use, and density
- dealing with housing and its production
- dealing with economic development providing ecologically safe employment for the entire labor force, with minimal inequality
- dealing with health and mental health
- dealing with education
- dealing with issues of accessibility and transportation
- overcoming the failures of urban planning in the twentieth century (urban sprawl, congestion, crime, pollution, environmental degradation, class inequality, racial segregation)
- dealing with poverty, inequality, racial and religious disparities, and crime
- dealing with environmental protection

Overall, every process involved in growing urbanization also involves global environmental, economic, and social impacts (Stokols 2018; Gough 2017). Chopping down a tree to build a house has an influence on greenhouse gas emissions and natural resources. The lost tree no longer absorbs CO_2. The transport of construction materials has an impact on global warming and environmental resources. The ultimate occupants of the dwelling, through their need for heat, food, and their consumer behavior and travel behavior, have impacts on climate problems.

For urban population to grow by 2.5 billion people by 2050 clearly suggests a greatly expanded role for global, comprehensive, transdisciplinary urban planning—not only for those professionally trained but also for all configurations and disciplines of sustainable understanding and leadership: social, economic, psychological, and political.

References

Angel et al. 2016. *Atlas of Urban Expansion—2016 Edition, Volume 1: Areas and Densities*. New York: New York University; Nairobi: UN-Habitat; and Cambridge, MA: Lincoln Institute of Land Policy.

Bolan, R. S. 2017. *Urban Planning's Philosophical Entanglements: The Rugged Dialectical Path from Knowledge to Action*. New York: Routledge.

Banfield, E. C. 1959. "Ends and Means in Planning." *UNESCO International Social Science Journal* XI: 365–68.

Cesanek, W., V. Elmer, and J. Graeff. 2017. *Planners and Water*. PAS Report 588. American Planning Association.

Daly, H. 1996. *Beyond Growth: The Economics of Sustainable Development*. Boston: Beacon Press.

Dawson, A. 2017. *Extreme Cities: The Peril and Promise of Urban Life in the Age of Climate Change*. London: Verso.

Goodell, J. 2017. *The Water Will Come: Rising Seas, Sinking Cities and the Remaking of the Civilized World*. New York: Little Brown and Company.

Gough, I. 2017. *Heat, Greed and Human Need: Climate Change, Capitalism and Sustainable Wellbeing*. Cheltonham, UK: Edward Elgar Publishing.

McNeill, J. R., and P. Engelke. 2014. *The Great Acceleration: An Environmental History of the Anthropocene since 1945*. Cambridge, MA: Harvard University Press.

Muggah, R. 2017. "Where Are the World's Most Fragile Cities?" CityLab, November 17.

Nordhaus, William D. 2013. *The Climate Casino: Risk, Uncertainty, and Economics for a Warming World*. New Haven: Yale University Press.

Popper, K. 1945. *The Open Society and Its Enemies*. Princeton: Princeton University Press.

Stokols, D. 2018. *Social Ecology in the Digital Age: Solving Complex Problems in a Globalized World*. London, UK: Elsevier, Academic Press.

Chapter 3

The Rise of the Oligopoly Corporatist Economy

There is one significant group of dominant contributors to the planet Earth's Tragedy of the Commons—the contemporary global economy. The impact today has become more visible and has stimulated more concern since the end of World War II.

Economic growth started to become global in the 1970s. In the 1980s, less and less attention was given to antitrust laws. What began occurring were many mergers and acquisitions. As firms became larger, they bought smaller competitors and essentially began to aspire toward monopoly. Today in the global economy, there are many forms of oligopoly. Oligopoly leaders seek not only profits through greed (à la Adam Smith) but also *control through power*. This chapter will elaborate what I describe as the oligopoly corporatist economy. The use of oligopoly corporatist power to minimize government regulation has become dominant internationally. From this dynamic, we are experiencing much stronger corporate control over the urban development process.

What Is an Oligopoly?

The website Investopedia has an excellent definition of what constitutes a corporate oligopoly:

> Oligopoly is a market structure in which a small number of firms has the large majority of market share. An oligopoly is similar to a monopoly, except that rather than one firm, two or more firms dominate the market. There is no precise upper limit to the number of firms in an oligopoly, but the number must be low enough that the actions of one firm significantly impact and influence the others. (http://www.investopedia.com/terms/o/oligopoly.asp#ixzz4ujl1nydH)

A large majority of market share provides each company in an oligopoly the ability to manipulate pricing through control of the supply. The ability to manipulate price carries with it the ability to control each firm's profit margin. Oligopolies also show characteristics that provide significant obstacles for new companies to enter their market. Another common characteristic of an oligopoly is for companies to cooperate, or collude, in their control of price and supply. While this technically is illegal under US antitrust law, price-fixing is quite common in the practice of oligopolies.

Underlying this pursuit of oligopolies is behavior moving beyond mere seeking of profit. Power and control are also sought. The following from investopedia.com describes the motivation for market power:

> Market power refers to a company's relative ability to manipulate the price of an item in the marketplace by manipulating the level of supply, demand or both. A company with substantial market power has the ability to manipulate market price and thereby control its profit margin, and possibly the ability to increase obstacles to potential new entrants into the market. Firms that have market power are often described as "price makers" because they have the ability to establish or adjust the marketplace price of an item without relinquishing market share. (http://www.investopedia.com/terms/m/market-power.asp#ixzz4wpVdLY5b)

On the same website is a description of a major behavioral aspect of oligopolies, the power of collusion:

> Collusion may occur in several ways, typically producing the same end result – a party, often consumers, being disadvantaged in some particular manner. One of the most common forms of collusion is price fixing. This occurs when there is a small number of companies in the marketplace, commonly referred to as an oligopoly, essentially offering the same product, and agreement is made to collaborate and set a minimum price. Similarly, companies may collude by setting a maximum price for supplies that they purchase. Companies may collude to eliminate or reduce competition. (http://www.investopedia.com/terms/c/collusion.asp#ixzz4wpX8c79c)

In this twenty-first century, creation of oligopolies has taken place on a worldwide basis. Many foreign corporations have purchased American corporations and vice versa. One example is the merger of two automobile companies: Fiat (in Italy) with Chrysler in the United States. In recent years, we have also seen the Anglo-Swedish company AstraZeneca purchase MedImmune of Maryland; the Taiwanese computer giant Acer bought the California computer company Gateway; and the Brazilian meatpacker JBS-Friboi acquired the Colorado-based Swift & Company (Lynn 2010, chapter 1).

> The most popular geographic targets for U.S. companies in the first half of 2013 were Brazil (25 deals), India (18 deals), South American countries excluding Brazil (15), South and East Asia (15), and Central America and Caribbean (14). (https://www.forbes.com/sites/kenrapoza/2013/09/15/u-s-companies-buying-up-foreign-competition/#3f0e257adb01)

The global importance of the corporatist world can be quickly viewed in the map shown in figure 3.1. This map shows the geographic spread of Fortune 500 corporations.

Figure 3.1. Fortune 500 global companies—2017

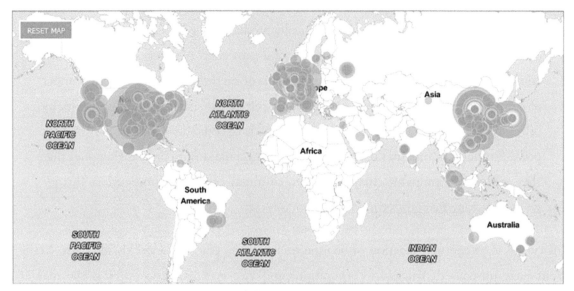

Historical Patterns Leading to a Corporatist Dominance

The corporation has a long history in the developed world. This is notable in the United Kingdom, the USA, and Europe.[11] As industrialization moved forward in the nineteenth century, some economic activity moved toward monopolistic tendencies. The United States Congress passed antitrust legislation beginning with an act in 1890, followed by additional action in 1907 and 1914. These actions were to stop monopolistic tendencies in the provision of railroads, energy, and banking. Some monopolies were allowed, particularly those of utilities. Thus, electricity and telephone monopolies were allowed but subject to strict state and government control and limited regional markets.

---

[11] For a strong, detailed history of global corporatism, see Robert Kuttner (2018), *Can Democracy Survive Global Capitalism?* (New York: W.W. Norton Company).

The 1920s, the flapper age, saw a prosperous economy with growth of corporate entities. This, however, led to the Depression of the 1930s that saw many business failures and high levels of unemployment. The Roosevelt years in this decade saw a period of strong government intervention, particularly in providing broad employment through the WPA program, the Civil Conservation Corps program, arts programs, and other areas of opportunity. In fact, more than eleven million government jobs were created during the Depression (Wolff 2016). In housing, mortgage programs were broadened, and a secondary housing market was created, thereby assuring government-provided mortgage banking liquidity. There was general economic growth until 1937 when a second milder depression occurred, yet economic growth continued at a slower pace (Kuttner 2018).

The post–World War I depression years in Europe were distinguished by the rise of strong dictatorships in Russia and Germany. The Soviet Union first emerged in 1917 under the leadership of Lenin, but the rise of Stalin began in 1922, and he became the supreme dictator in 1941 (Wikipedia). Stalin made the Soviet Union a strong world power. In Germany, Hitler rose to power in 1933 and became dictator in 1934. While Hitler and Stalin had a nonaggression pact, this soon collapsed. In both these countries, a strong dictatorial focus on armament production meant a form of economic growth. There has even been evidence of American corporate help in creating these militaristic economies, particularly through the provision of petroleum (Mayer 2016; Sampson 1975). Japan, of course, had its own military economy while pursuing its invasions of the Philippines and China in the 1930s and its attack on Pearl Harbor in 1941.

World War II altered the economy as production of civilian goods shifted to wartime equipment. This meant that capitalist producers of civilian goods became under government control for military equipment. The military active duty draft meant a shortage of labor for domestic production, so that women became a strong part of the World War II labor force.

The postwar 1950s and 1960s saw strong economic growth under the Bretton Woods Agreement, with particular evidence of corporate growth. The 1970s saw the beginning of a global corporatist world. American corporations began setting up operations in Europe, Latin America, East Asia, and the Middle East.

One of the earliest oligopolies was found in the petroleum industry. This was well described by Arthur Sampson in his 1975 book, *The Seven Sisters*.

The latter 1970s saw opportunity to produce goods overseas at strikingly low labor costs (Bluestone and Harrison 1982). This was highly advantageous in garment manufacturing. In addition, by the 1980s, it was close to impossible to buy a television set that had been manufactured in the US. This was also the beginning of significant loss of jobs for American workers.

The key historical period leading to today's corporate world was generally the Reagan-Thatcher years, 1980–1990. This was the period where economic theory was broadly deflected away from Keynesian theory (as was exemplified in the Bretton Woods Agreement) to supply-side economics. This shift was in response to the period of high inflation rates (stagflation) and the wage-price spiral in the 1970 Nixon-Ford-Carter years. These issues applied to the US and European and Latin American countries. As Robert Kuttner explained, "The return to market fundamentalism was supposed to energize economic growth. It did not. It did restore both inequality and instability, with political repercussions to follow" (Kuttner 2018, Kindle location 1370).

Kuttner further elaborates:

> Very high interest rates in the US reverberated throughout the system, doing further damage to the postwar economic system, its political footings, and the security of working people, and creating catastrophic losses in Latin America." (Kuttner 2018, Kindle location 1376)

Thus, in 1980, there was a major shift back to laissez-faire, or what is currently referred to as neoliberalism. The traces of global financial regulation were pretty much removed. This shift affected not only developed countries; major economic problems also arose in Latin America and East Asia. The roles of the International Monetary Fund and the World Bank were reduced to laissez-faire statistical assistance and advisory bodies.

In the United States, antitrust laws were largely ignored. The period of 1984 to 1990 saw growth in significant mergers and acquisitions, leading toward beginning oligopoly characteristics. In the 1990s, there was some retrenchment from mergers and acquisitions, but with the twenty-first century, this activity increased once again. The year 2016 saw a new global high in mergers and acquisitions.

Contemporary Concerns Involving Economic Theory

The economy of the twenty-first century is new. While its history primarily evolved over the last half of the twentieth century, much of what goes on today has moved far beyond the events taking place in those previous years.

For students studying economics, universities and colleges still offer courses in microeconomics and macroeconomics (with the underlying ideal of laissez-faire). These come from a rather simplistic set of assumptions concerning the rationality of individuals both as consumers and as owners of business. Economic theory was strongly based on Adam Smith's concept of the invisible hand, a term that is a metaphor for how, in a free market economy, self-interested individuals (pursuing the behavior of greed) operate within a larger system of mutual interdependence, yielding the promotion of general benefit of society at large. The concept of trade and market exchange automatically moved self-interest toward socially desirable goals and thus the primary justification for the laissez-faire economic philosophy. The invisible hand is, in effect, the deep assumption lying behind classical economic theory.[12]

Economists have debated this for some time. An early critique was that of Joseph Stiglitz, where he pointed out the existence of *externalities*—market transactions where the actions of one seller dealing with one buyer has impacts on others for which the seller and buyer do not pay, or for which those outside the transaction are not compensated. However, as Nobel Prize winner William Nordhaus notes, "The unregulated invisible hand sets the prices incorrectly when there are important externalities" (Nordhaus 2013, 18). Probably the most important externality in the modern world is that economic activity produces air and water pollution and climate warming.[13] Another example of externality is that of a company opening a factory in another

---

[12] An interesting modern interpretation of the invisible hand is provided by Matthias Ruth (*Advanced Introduction to Ecological Economics*, 2018, page 18). He states: "Rather, markets are social institutions as well, where power, preferential access tradition, seniority and chance are the fingers that make up the invisible hand."

[13] Some contemporary personalities highlight this conflict. Supporters of coal, oil, and gas interests in the world refuse to acknowledge the pollution caused by their activity. This is not only their belief but also that of the head of the EPA and the current president of the USA, who have introduced policies that ignore the externality of pollution.

country with lower costs of labor, resulting in the company's increase in profits. The key externality, of course, is the loss of jobs in the hometown of the company (Wolff 2016).

Changes in economic theory have come into being. There is, for example, the emergence of a new field linking economics and psychology. Other studies of rationality have also been involved (Bolan 1999). In short, the notion of simple rationality in economic behavior has shown to be naïve and often erroneous. What is most noticeable today is the pursuit not only of greed but also power. A corporatist economy has gone beyond a simple pursuit of profit. The corporate world is very much involved in minimizing the basic regulatory rules of market behavior imposed by government or other institutions. Chapter 4 will discuss how this expands into controlling governmental institutions.

A key problem from this is that theories of microeconomics and macroeconomics are no longer truly relevant. Historically, macroeconomics has never really worked out. There is a long history of economic growth followed by economic depression. Economic theory has generally failed in any effort to prevent depression. Today, there is significant change in the economic world.

When supply-side theory or neoliberalism came to the fore at the end of the twentieth century, there was argument that leaving corporate leadership minimally regulated would positively result in trickle-down theory, where the poor would gain in labor opportunity and prosperity. The evidence of the twenty-first century is exactly the opposite. If anything, a prospering economy has meant a "trickle-up theory" for the well-to-do, resulting in significantly growing inequality (Pozner and Weyl 2018, 8). When we combine this with the substantial growth of world urban population discussed in the previous chapter, many questions about the future arise.

In effect, while we tend to believe that we have a free market economy, we actually have moved to a global "oligopolistic-corporate" economy. In this movement, many of the basic assumptions and concepts of traditional economic analysis are no longer relevant.

Look first at microeconomics. The following chart (figure 3.2) tends to portray the basic operation of supply and demand in a free market economy. With everyone acting in terms of utility maximization through rational action, we see the demand for a product set up by a demand curve. If the price is very high, demand is low; if the price is very low, demand is high. The business unit is involved in the various costs of producing their product. In meeting increasing supplies of the product, the graph depicts a supply curve. At the intersection of supply and demand, we have the price of the transaction—the invisible hand at work. There is increasing evidence, however, that as corporations increase power and control of their markets, they exercise control over both supply and demand and thereby control of price.

Figure 3.2. What is happening in microeconomics?

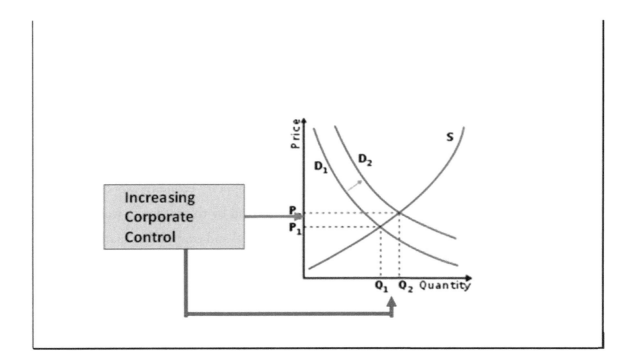

We have many instances where the price of products is not determined in the fashion of microeconomics (or the invisible hand) but more in terms of the control by the corporate producer (or the producer oligopoly). This has received publicity in popular media in recent times. One of the most obvious examples is in the pharmaceutical field. In the United States, customers have no role in the establishment of prices for medicine (customers also have little role in the price of health insurance or health care). As one reads the rest of this chapter, it will become clear that in several corporate fields, consumers have next to no voice in market prices.

Macroeconomics is the theoretical overview of the free-market operations of microeconomics. It is an inclusive broad view of the entire economy, including analyzing the relationships between businesses (corporations), governments and households. Macroeconomics explores different all-encompassing types of markets, such as the financial market, and the labor market. With overall labor market earnings, workers purchase necessities from the commodity market and/or put savings into the banks of the financial market. Business demands labor and pays wages. Governments tax everybody, but then transfer services and/or benefits to everyone (highways, schools, police and fire departments, water supply, etc.). In addition, foreign dimension involves imports and exports. With the "invisible hand," everyone presumably gets the social benefits that they want as the circulation takes place with no real exercise of control or power (with the possible exception of government sitting in the center of the system with taxing authority and (perhaps) limited forms of regulatory authority).

Figure 3.3 is my cartoon depicting the actual way the contemporary economy works. In this diagram, the dominance of oligopolies means there is nearly total command by the corporate world. The corporate world has become the major force—even extending to the financial and commodity markets and including powerful forces of the international market. My cartoon also indicates that households and governments are also fully under the control of the corporate world.

The earliest oligopoly tended to focus on energy, particularly coal, oil, and petroleum (Sampson 1975), and this remains a dominant oligopoly to this day. Oligopolies exist in the commodity market with big-box retailing exercising control of both supply and prices. Oligopolies are in the financial market with a few big banks in dominant locations in New York, London, Paris, and Tokyo. Oligopolies also exist in the productive manufacturing markets, as will be discussed below. Oligopolies are also dominant in electronic communications and artificial intelligence. Finally, international markets are truly powerful in the contemporary scene. Thus, the dashed red circle portrays the total dominance of combined avarice and power in today's corporatist economy—not the invisible hand influencing greed alone. Power and control are the dominant psychological marks.

Figure 3.3

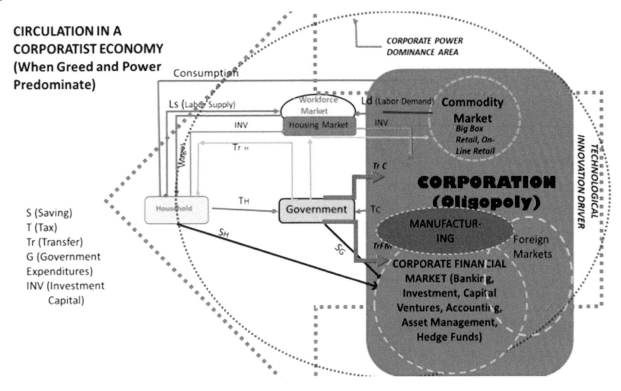

CIRCULATION IN A CORPORATIST ECONOMY (When Greed and Power Predominate)

S (Saving)
T (Tax)
Tr (Transfer)
G (Government Expenditures)
INV (Investment Capital)

Table 3.1 shows a list of the key oligopolies present today, together with a list of the prominent firms involved in each. This list is derived from numerous website sources as well as data provided by contemporary mass media sources. The text following will examine a few of the more prominent oligopolies.

Table 3.1. Major oligopolies in the United States and abroad—2017

Major Oligopolies	Top Firms
Agricultural seeds, fertilizers	DowDuPont, Monsanto-Bayer, Syngenta, Cargill
Agricultural equipment	John Deere, CNH, AGCO, CLAAS, Same Deutz-Fahr, Kubota
Airline services	American, Delta, United, Southwest
Airplane manufacturing	Boeing, Airbus
Automobiles	General Motors, Ford, Toyota, Honda, Chrysler, Nissan, Kai
Banking, finance	Bank of America, Wells Fargo, JP Morgan, Citi Bank, Goldman Sachs, Capital One, Chinese banks
Big-box retail	Walmart, Target, Amazon, Costco
Computers	Intel, Dell, Hewlett-Packard, Apple, Lenovo, Gl
Communications	Google, Facebook, Amazon, Comcast, Verizon, T-Mobile, AT&T, Sprint[2]
Energy—petroleum	Sinopec (China), China National Petroleum, Royal Dutch Shell, Exxon Mobile, Chevron
Food	Tyson, 3G Capital, Berkshire Hathaway, Nestle, General Mills, Roark Capital
Health insurance	Anthem, United Health Care, CIGNA, Aetna, Blue Cross-Blue Shield
Military armaments	BAE Systems, Northrup Grumman, Lockheed Martin, General Dynamics, Boeing
Pharmaceuticals	Johnson & Johnson, McKesson, Novartis, Pfizer, Hoffman-LaRoche, Sanofi, Merck, GlaxoSmithKline, Eli Lilly, AbbVire
Retail pharmacy	CVS, Walgreens
Rental cars	Avis, Hertz, Enterprise
Steel, aluminum	US Steel, Nippon, JFE, Sahsteel, Tata, Alcoa

The Coal-Oil Oligopoly

The coal-oil oligopoly is likely the oldest, going back to the early twentieth century. It is the oligopoly that has been the most significant foundation of modern urbanization. However, it has had significant variability over the years. It still exists, but many of the top companies have changed through mergers, acquisitions, and the discovery of new resource locations. In the beginning of the twentieth century, the United States was the world leader in oil resources. At the time of Sampson's book (1975), the formation of OPEC had taken place, with the primary source of petroleum in the Middle East. Today, however, the source of oil has become much more diverse, with major companies now emerging in many different countries around the world, such as Mexico, Venezuela, Russia, China, Canada, and the United States.

Nonetheless, ecological economist Tim Jackson notes in his most recent book:

> Annual carbon dioxide emissions from the burning of fossil fuels (and from industry) have more than tripled since 1965. Even within the last decade, emissions have been growing at more than 2 per cent per year on average. (Jackson 2017, 90)

With the diverse sources of raw materials, the traditional oligopoly companies have not been able to prevent competition from increasing. Gasoline for automobiles, for example, has very much returned to Adam Smith's invisible hand, so that prices are strongly influenced by worldwide supply and demand. Gas prices became very high in 2008 but then got much lower in 2010. Prices have remained at relatively low levels in the last few years, although increases may vary on a seasonal, timely basis. Low price levels also mean the enlargement of the externality of emission production.

There are factors at work in the world economy today that might pose significant problems for this oligopoly. Coal and oil (along with natural gas) used to be the key source for heating buildings and providing electricity, but there is increasing attention to solar and wind energy for these purposes.[14] Energy for

---

[14] Solar, wind, and hydro energy sources have become competitive market-wise. However, their use is still a minority contribution for energy, with considerable variability across the world (and across different states in the US).

automobiles and trucks is still dominated by petroleum. More attention is being given to the development of electric or hybrid vehicles, but progress at the time of this writing is slow.

The overall problem with the coal-oil oligopoly really focuses on the extreme environmental externalities that become more and more important. The initial operation of transforming crude oil into petrochemicals releases toxins into the atmosphere that are dangerous for human and ecosystem health. In addition, burning gasoline releases CO_2, so that auto and truck use contributes significantly to local pollution as well as to greenhouse gases, thereby increasing global warming. The rising use of natural gas does not provide the benefits the energy oligopolists claim. Methane is a major global emission, even more detrimental than CO_2.

The spilling of oil also causes great environmental damage. Large oil spills sometimes occur during drilling, transport, and use, which of course affects the surrounding environment. Large oil spills such as the 1989 *Exxon Valdez* in Alaska or the 2010 BP *Deepwater Horizon* in the Gulf of Mexico are given extensive media coverage, but most of the oil spilled into ecosystems is from oil that leaks from cars, airplanes, and boats, as well as illegal dumping. Recent years have also seen significant spills from deteriorating pipelines.

While petroleum has become a much larger oligopoly with many more firms in many more countries, the wealth in the field is still predominate and has led to significant political influence in the United States and other countries.

The following table provides a list of the top ten international oil companies ranked by the amount of revenue they earned in 2015. China has become dominant in the oligopoly. This ranking has changed over time. For example, at one point, Russia was one of the top oil-producing countries, but in 2015, they were not at the top. The European companies are still prominent, but they rely strongly on the Middle East. Significant oil has been found in central US and Canada, and the growing dominance of China is evident from these recent earnings.

Clearly, this oligopoly is of extreme importance in relation to planet Earth's Tragedy of the Commons. It is of major importance in global warming and in world urban functioning (heating/cooling, electricity, transportation). Solar and wind energy help, but they still need significantly more competitive strength. The use of petroleum in transportation, however, shows few immediate signs of alternative means of moving about locally or globally.

Table 3.2. Largest international oil companies by revenue

Company Name	Country	Revenue 2015 (US$ millions)
Saudi Aramco	Saudi Arabia	$455.49
Sinopec	China	448.00
China National Petroleum Corporation	China	428.62
Petro China	China	367.98
Exxon Mobil	United States	268.90
Royal Dutch Shell	Netherlands and UK	265.00
Kuwait Petroleum Corporation	Kuwait	251.94
BP	United Kingdom	222.80
Total SA	France	212.00
Lukoil	Russia	144.17

(Source: https://en.wikipedia.org/wiki/List_of_largest_oil_and_gas_companies_by_revenue.)

The Automobile Oligopoly

One of the telltale anecdotes illustrating the interdependence and collusion of the automobile oligopoly is a quote from the CEO of Ford Motor Company during the Great Recession when General Motors and Chrysler were on the verge of bankruptcy. There was a proposal before Congress to have the United States government bailout General Motors. Barry Lynn quoted the Ford CEO, Alan Mulally:

> A remarkable statement made by Ford CEO Alan Mulally in the late fall of 2008. During his testimony on Capitol Hill, Mulally asked Congress to provide loans to keep his rivals alive. The automotive industry, Mulally explained, is *"uniquely interdependent."* This was particularly true, he said, "with respect to our supply base, *with more than 90 percent commonality among our suppliers.* Should one of the other domestic companies declare bankruptcy, the effect on Ford's production operations would be felt within days—if not hours … Without parts for the just-in-time inventory system, Ford plants would not be able to produce vehicles. (Lynn 2010, Kindle location 190) (My emphasis.)

This reflects an important transformation that took place in the automobile manufacturing industry a few years back. Historically, auto manufacturers manufactured their own parts and assembled those parts to complete their finished products. In the late 1990s and early 2000s, the general adoption of the just-in-time inventory system meant that individual auto producers purchased parts from other producers (often in other countries with much lower wages and therefore much lower prices) and, with robotic help, primarily produces only *assembled* cars in their up-to-date factories, minimizing real estate space for parts and supplies.[15]

---

[15] One of the most difficult aspects of this procedure came from the production of faulty airbags primarily from a Japanese firm. This had an impact on all automobile companies.

This is a good example of how oligopolies can collude to minimize production costs without lowering sales costs. As a result, with government help, General Motors is back in business and doing fine, along with the other international automobile manufacturers, including Ford, Toyota, Honda, Fiat-Chrysler, and Nissan.

The Communications Oligopoly

The communications oligopoly is considerably more complex. There is little question of the power of Google in the communications field. Additionally, Facebook and Apple are right up there with Google. They control the basics of social communications. They have also taken control relatively quickly. At the beginning of the twenty-first century, they were brand-new firms. However, the relationships of electronic communications today involve their control of smaller firms with specialized products.

Communications in the contemporary world began with the development of computers progressing from the days of the early massive instruments (that would occupy a whole room or even a whole building in the 1960s and 1970s) to the advent of the small, personal desktop computers (in the 1970s) and then, with the introduction of the internet, extending to laptops, tabloids, the cell phone, and the smartphone.

One significant characteristic today is that it is very difficult to buy a computer that does not have a microprocessor manufactured by Intel. This is a near monopoly. The purchase of a personal computer is possible through a wide range of domestic and international manufacturers, yet Dell, Hewlett-Packard, Apple, and Lenovo fundamentally dominate computer sales, both PCs and laptops. Microsoft enjoys a nearly complete dominance in the provision of fundamental software, providing ease in use of computers by most buyers (Windows 10).[16]

As technology became more personal (and significantly smaller yet more powerful in communication diversity), an oligopoly in direct person-to-person, smartphone capability boils down to four primary companies providing this service: Verizon, T-Mobile, AT&T, and Sprint. In April 2018, T-Mobile and

---

[16] Those of us who are aged can remember using a computer before the availability of Windows. This meant being able to write your own programs so that the computer could give you answers. Windows is a very near monopoly.

Sprint announced their intention to merge. In addition, three companies dominate the manufacturing of cell phones: Apple, Google, and Samsung.

There is also evidence of oligopoly in broadcast communications. The Sinclair broadcast company is dominant in the ownership nationally of *local* radio and TV stations. It is also noted for lack of political neutrality; it extensively promotes right wing ideology at local levels. Comcast and Time Warner dominate cable television, along with the Canadian firm of Rogers.

Time Warner is a corporate leader in broadcast communications, owning HBO, Warner Bros., CNN, TBS, and TNT. Another major oligopolistic proposal was the merger of Time Warner with AT&T. On June 12, 2018, this merger was approved by a federal court. It has also been reported that Rupert Murdoch has sold much of his Twenty-First-Century Fox Empire to the Disney Company.

Comcast Corporation is the American global telecommunications conglomerate that is the largest broadcasting and cable television company in the world by revenue. It is the second-largest pay-TV company, largest cable TV company, and largest home internet service provider in the United States. Comcast is also the nation's third largest home (land) telephone service provider. As the owner of the international media company, NBC Universal (acquired in 2011), Comcast is a producer of feature films and television programs intended for theatrical exhibition and over-the-air and cable television broadcast.

Comcast operates over-the-air national broadcast network channels (NBC and Telemundo), multiple cable-only channels (including MSNBC, CNBC, USA Network, NBCSN, E!, and The Weather Channel, among others). Comcast owns the film production studio Universal Pictures, as well as Universal Parks & Resorts in Los Angeles, California; Orlando, Florida; and Osaka, Japan. Comcast owns Universal Studios Singapore, one of the four Universal operating theme parks. It is introducing new locations, such as Universal Studios Beijing. Comcast also has significant holdings in digital distribution, such as the Platform, acquired in 2006.

In December 2017, the Federal Communications Commission turned away from internet neutrality and succumbed to the powers of Comcast, AT&T, and Verizon. Former head of the Federal Communications Commission, Tom Wheeler, stated:

With this vote, the FCC walked away from over a decade of bipartisan efforts to oversee the fairness and openness of companies such as Comcast, AT&T, Charter, and Verizon. These four companies control over 75 percent of the residential internet access in America, usually through a local monopoly. Henceforth, they will be able to make their own rules, subject only to very limited after-the-fact review. (Brookings Brief Newsletter, December 15, 2017)

This is a good example of the power of oligopolies, not only in the marketplace but also in government regulation and oversight. This is covered in more detail in the next chapter.

The Pharmaceutical Oligopoly

Pharmaceutical companies benefited greatly from the Medicare Prescription Drug Modernization Act passed in December 2003. While the act promoted enhancement of senior Medicare, a critical provision was that the US government *could not* negotiate drug prices. While this has meant all other countries might negotiate pharmaceutical prices, in the United States, the drug companies have full control over pricing.

A recent survey of pharmaceutical pricing (July 1, 2017) by American Family Physicians, posted on their website (https://www.aafp.org/afp/2017/0701/p20.html), found dramatic recent increases in pricing in the United States. A few of these increases have received considerable media attention. However, the findings of the American Family Physicians indicate that the practice can be widespread and can be especially difficult for low- and middle-income families as well as insurance providers. The power of this oligopoly most dramatically shows up in serious illness situations.

A patient with asthma can expect to pay $310 for a single inhaler of fluticasone/salmeterol (Advair) in the United States, whereas the same product costs $35 in France. Also, for one with asthma, a longtime dosage going back years is adrenaline (known today as epinephrine). A single dose in 2011 was $50, and in 2017, the price was $300. A more recent drug for asthma is known as Isoproterenol, and it changed from $180 per dose to $1,472 per dose overnight. A drug for diabetes (Nitroprusside) increased from $215 per dose to $1,346 per dose overnight. A drug for rheumatoid arthritis (penicillamine) increased from $9 per pill to $1,200 per pill overnight. An ointment for eczema (Aloquin) increased from $30 to $3,600 for a 60 g tube. Drug treatment for leukemia over a one-year period went from $124,000 to $299,000. For toxoplasmosis, the price increased from $13.50 per tablet to $750 per tablet.

One price increase receiving a high level of publicity in the United States involved the drug known as EpiPens. In 2015, Mylan (a subsidiary of Pfizer) had about $1.5 billion in sales of EpiPens, and those sales accounted for 40 percent of Mylan's profit. Mylan had maintained about a 90 percent market share since it had acquired the product and had continually raised the price of EpiPens, starting in 2009 when the wholesale price of two EpiPens was about $100. By July 2013, the price was about $265; in May 2015, it was around $461; in May 2016, the price rose again to around $609, around a 500 percent jump from the price in 2009!

CBS *60 Minutes* exposed the corporate distribution of opioid painkillers in October 2017 with a follow-up disclosure in December 2017. Congress passed a bill prohibiting government agencies from regulating the supply of these drugs, despite the recognition that this drug was the cause of an emergency national problem of drug overdose. In November 2017, President Trump declared a national health emergency to tackle the opioid epidemic, yet the funds available at that time in that fiscal track only amounted to $56,000—clearly inadequate funding for taking on a national epidemic.[17] A recent report in the *Nation* magazine website (December 15, 2017) described a price hike for a drug designed to tackle drug overuse.

> The largest price hike was for Evzio, an auto-injector device designed for easy use by laypersons. In 2014, a two-dose package of Evzio, manufactured by kaléo, cost $690. As of 2016, it cost $4,500. That's more than a 500 percent increase.

Pharmaceutical companies contend that their pricing is based upon their need to invest in research and development for improving medical care. This tends to overlook that most of the medical research takes place in universities and prominent health care centers. What is also of primary importance is that pharmaceutical

---

[17] A primary maker of OxyContin—generally the major creator of the opioid epidemic (McLellan)—is finally in 2019 being challenged in court.

companies spend more on marketing and advertising than they do on research. Money is also spent on direct marketing to doctors, and companies hire doctors to help in the marketing process.

Table 3.3 shows the recent revenues, expenditures, and profits of the top ten pharmaceutical companies providing medicine to the United States for the year 2013. Gross revenue for all firms was over $400 billion, with the top company earning over $70 billion. What is more important, however, was that the top companies spent more on marketing and sales than on research. For all ten top companies, the average of marketing and sales expenditures exceeded research costs by 1.5 times. These ten companies had an average profit margin of close to 20 percent, with one firm enjoying a profit margin of 43 percent.

This report from the American Family Association gives an excellent picture of the pharmaceutical oligopoly. Unfortunately, there is little reporting of one of the top sellers of pharmaceuticals in the United States. Being a corporation in the pharmaceutical oligopoly is clearly being in a superlative controlling economic situation.[18] Consumers have no power; if they are ill and need a pharmaceutical, they pay the price or continue their illness.

Table 3.3. Pharmaceutical spending and revenue—2013

Revenue Rank	Company	Total Revenue $Billion	R&D Spending $Billion	Sales/Marketing Spending $Billion	Marketing/ Research Ratio	Profit $Billion	Profit Margin %
1	Johnson & Johnson (US)	71.3	8.2	17.5	2.13	13.8	19
2	Novartis (US)	58.8	9.9	14.6	1.47	9.2	16
3	Pfizer (US)	51.6	6.6	11.4	1.73	22	43
4	Hoffman-La Roche (Swiss)	50.3	9.3	9.0	0.97	12	24
5	Sanofi (France)	44.4	6.3	9.1	1.44	8.5	11
6	Merck (US)	44.0	7.5	9.5	1.27	4.4	10
7	GSK (UK)	41.4	5.3	9.9	1.87	8.5	21
8	AstraZeneca (UK)	25.7	4.3	7.3	1.70	2.6	10
9	Eli Lilly (US)	23.1	5.5	5.7	1.04	4.7	20
10	AbbVire (US)	18.8	2.9	4.3	1.48	4.1	22
	TOTAL ALL FIRMS	429.4	65.8	98.3 Average : 1.51		89.8 Average 19.1	

Source: Global Data: found on http://www.bbc.com/news/business-28212223

---

[18] While working on the text of this chapter, it was announced that CVS Pharmacy will purchase Aetna Insurance Company for $69 billion. In the contemporary world of mergers and acquisitions, this seems likely to be approved by federal regulators. The two firms are not in direct competition with each other, even though both hold dominant positions in the overall health field.

Military and Civilian Armaments Oligopoly

The production of military arms represents a significant oligopoly with considerable global marketing. Many arms manufacturers exist throughout the world, but only a few dominate. The American companies account for more than 60 percent of worldwide sales. Military arms producers focus on military forces for many global national governments. However, some of the arms manufacturers may also produce goods for groups other than governmental military organizations. Clearly, corporate interests in creating global products for making war are strong.

The largest manufacturers today reflect the nature of modern warfare. More battles are fought remotely through air surveillance and strikes than in on-the-ground human combat. As a result, the largest companies are among the leading aerospace companies. Surveillance and battlefield communications are increasingly important in modern warfare, so that the largest companies also have significant electronics divisions. The largest manufacturers are also involved in the manufacture of naval vessels.

Sales of small arms in the United States are quite significant. While there are many such manufacturers throughout the world, three dominate: Smith & Wesson, Colt, and Remington.

Perhaps the biggest producer of military arms is a firm known as BAE systems. The company is based in London but has operations in forty countries around the world. Its largest markets are the defense departments in the United Kingdom, the United States, Saudi Arabia, Australia, and India. Arms sales are 95 percent of its total sales. BAE produces virtually all forms of military equipment: aircraft, naval vessels, munitions, and electronic equipment.

Other major United States corporations include Northrop Grumman (arms sales are 81 percent of all sales), Lockheed Martin (arms sales are 75 percent of total), General Dynamics (arms sales are 74 percent), and Boeing (arms sales are 49 percent of total sales). The military oligopoly is not truly featured in public mass media. Yet it is clearly the largest contemporary manufacturing operation in the world. The number of soldiers and sailors serving a country clearly does not measure the size of military operations in contemporary times. Present-day military operations are highly mechanized as well as dependent on communications technology and robotic drones (noted in chapter 5). Manufacturing of this is extremely important, given the significant monetary investment resources that are involved, as well as the important labor force needs in the manufacturing sector.

More broadly, we do not live in a peaceful world. Possible war threats create significant consumption of earth resources and labor inputs that impact the Tragedy of the Commons. Ironically, the United States and United Kingdom see the military as a world market product. As noted by Jeffrey Sachs, "The United States seems content to pump the Middle East and other regions to the brim with armaments, as long as they are American armaments" (Sachs 2017, Kindle location 1494).

Food Oligopolies

Food is becoming increasingly under the influence of corporate oligopolies. As long ago as I can remember, there were large producers of certain types of food products: Coca-Cola, Pepsi-Cola, Nestlé, Hershey, and so on. In the last few years, food more broadly has become increasingly under the control of corporate power. This has its beginnings in the basics of agriculture with seed and fertilizer dominated by Monsanto, DuPont, and Dow corporations. In fact, on August 31, 2017, DuPont and Dow successfully merged to form the DowDuPont Corporation. Other US corporations influencing agriculture include Cargill and Archer Daniels Midlands.

In terms of packaged food products, there are many examples of corporatist oligopoly domination. Lynn described one such example:

> One of the most dramatic such roll-ups of power took place in dairy; Dean Foods and Dairy Farmers of America now split roughly 80 percent of the business. Given that the two work together in more or less open collusion, they form what in essence is a single private government that determines who gets to milk cows in America and who doesn't. (Lynn 2010, 150)

Another such area of domination is in the production of packaged chickens and chicken parts. Four companies control much of the distribution of these food parts: Tyson, Pilgrims Pride, Koch Foods, and

Perdue (Harvestland). These four companies enjoy 98 percent of the sales of chicken and have a domineering role in controlling the costs and operations of small chicken farmers in almost all the United States. These four companies are also dominant in determining chicken prices. Tyson is also a prevailing owner of numerous other food companies.

One investment firm has been instrumental in creating mergers in the food industry. Known as 3G Capital, this firm owns Restaurant Brands International, one of the world's largest quick-service restaurant companies with approximately $23 billion in system sales and more than eighteen thousand restaurants in one hundred countries. Restaurant Brands International owns two of the world's most prominent and iconic quick-service restaurant brands: Tim Hortons and Burger King.

Today, 3G Capital is a multibillion-dollar Brazilian investment firm with offices in New York, Rio de Janeiro, and Sao Paulo. The firm has also joined with the Berkshire Hathaway Corporation in many acquisitions. They also purchased and merged Kraft Foods and Heinz foods in 2015. They have also been involved in creating AbinBev, a conglomerate of beer companies in 150 countries throughout the world (including Anheuser Bush, Corona, Modelo, and Stella Artois).

True Dominance: The Berkshire Hathaway Corporation

Finally, one of the biggest corporations in the world is the Berkshire Hathaway Corporation. This company holds full or partial ownership in sixty-three corporations, predominantly in the United States. The company wholly owns the following corporations: GEICO, BNSF Railway, Lubrizol, Fruit of the Loom, Helzberg Diamonds, FlightSafety International, Pampered Chef, and NetJets. Berkshire Hathaway holds stock ownership in a diverse range of businesses, including confectionery, retail, railroad, home furnishings, encyclopedias, vacuum cleaners, jewelry sales, newspaper publishing, manufacture and distribution of uniforms, and several regional electric and gas utilities (http://www.berkshirehathaway.com/subs/sublinks.html).

Of interest to the urban planning profession is one area where Berkshire Hathaway holds important power involving home sales, mortgages, land titles, and home insurance. In September 2017, the firms of Long & Foster and Home Services Companies were merged. This linked two wholly owned Berkshire Hathaway companies. Long and Foster is headquartered in Virginia, and Home Services Companies is in Minnesota. Because of the merger, these combined companies will operate in thirty eastern and Midwest states. Thus, Berkshire Hathaway will have a strong role in real estate housing development in a large portion of the United States (*Minneapolis Star Tribune*, September 8, 2017, D1, D2).

The Banking and Finance Oligopoly

The final oligopoly I will call to your attention to is that involving banking, financial and investment firms – probably the most powerful set of corporations in today's world environment. (Harvey, 2010, chapter 2) This power is derived from dominating world financial transactions. As I tried to show in my cartoon in Figure 3.4, finance corporations are indeed the dominant corporations in today's oligopolistic corporatist economy. As financial transactions have increasingly become dominated by digital technology, this oligopoly controls not only majority of legal and appropriate transactions, but also money laundering, embezzling, and money hiding.

Historically, while banking was strictly controlled in the depression years of the 1930s, today it has emerged into one of the strongest economic activities that we experience. As an illustration, I bought my first house in the 1960s. However, in securing a mortgage, I could only work with a bank that was located in the same county where the house would be built. Today, one can apply for a home mortgage in any US or foreign bank including the top oligopolies no matter the location or neighborhood (or country) where you seek your mortgage.

As noted, this financing area of the economy has realized the most benefits from communication technology in the 21st century. These corporations have significant creativity with which they have been able to take very simple financial instruments (such as a mortgage) and link them together in ways that truly enrich their operations -- sometimes socially benefiting, but mostly personally benefiting.

Their operations, while creative, may often result in sometimes unethical or even illegal activity. Most everyone has some level of awareness of the major role of the mortgage sector in the Great Recession of 2007 to 2012. As one key report indicated, in the 1970s and early 1980s, investment banks converted from general partnerships, whose partners *had unlimited personal liability* for the debts of their firms, to corporations, whose managers *do not have personal liability* (Hill and Painter, 2016, Kindle location 142).

In effect, if a banker today creates a loss, he or she is not personally liable. In addition, if a banker creates an activity that ends up being determined as illegal, the fine is charged to the corporation, while the individual banker creating the illegal activity is not personally liable.

Financial corporations have both worldwide features as well as important roles within a nation state. From the Bankers Almanac website (https://accuity.com/resources/bank-rankings/), China is the country dominating world banking assets. China has the top four banks in the world and also has three additional banks with lower rank. The total assets of Chinese banks are $16 trillion in assets. The top banks of the United States are also ranked highly in world banking with J.P. Morgan Chase, Wells Fargo, Bank of America, and Citibank in this list – all totaling close to $7 trillion in assets. Also dominating in the list are banks in the Japan ($6.8 trillion), UK ($5.5 trillion), France ($5 trillion), and Germany ($1.7 trillion). What the Bankers Almanac does not show is the degree to which these banks individually operate worldwide.

The largest banks in the United States also operate throughout the world. From Wikipedia, it appears that Wells Fargo had operations in 35 countries in 2018. JP Morgan Chase had operations in more than 20 countries. Bank of America is in more than 40 countries (together with partner Merrill Lynch). One city that features housing foreign banks is Hong Kong.

This sector in the economy has many variations. Banks are often organized in holding companies that own and oversee many corporations. Today the term "bank" often refers to many different types of entities, including broker-dealers (brokerages), traditional investment banks, investment firms, asset managers, venture capitalists and other financial services entities, as well as depository and lending institutions. (Hill and Painter, 2016, Kindle location 290). The finance oligopolies are not just concerned with personal checking and savings accounts. This is an arena of organizations dealing with the widest array of local and global monetary transactions – including transactions involving the firms of other oligopolies that we have described above.

Thus, finance is an oligopoly of very dominant power. Its control over the major monetary transactions on the world scale suggests that it is one of the most important areas for governmental control.[19] This has

---

[19] A recent case, reported in the New York Times from August 2018 to November 2018, involves a major corruption scandal of hundreds of millions of dollars involving the bank Goldman Sachs in Malaysia.

tended to be the case historically, and this is the economic area that tends to dominate efforts at governmental lobbying and limiting governmental regulation. Banking is clearly an economic sector that has key roles in the urbanization process, and very much including housing. This is likely to continue with the urban growth described in Chapter 2. Clearly, in the basic processes of urban development today, this dominant oligopoly is a major factor in building cities today and highly likely in future years.

Cooperation, Collusion, and Other Interaction

Cooperation is present among businesses, both corporate and private, in the long history of the United States economy. It takes place organizationally within the following member groups: The National Association of Manufacturers, the US Chamber of Commerce, the Conference Board, the Business Council, the Committee for Economic Development, and the Business Roundtable. The National Association of Manufacturers originally formed in 1903. The US Chamber of Commerce is the largest group containing all types of American businesses. The chamber also works with state and local affiliates.

These organizations not only provide mechanisms for economic cooperation but also play a major role in looking after business interests involving government regulation, as will be discussed in more detail in the next chapter.

Corporate Interlocking

Since the 1980s and the growth of mergers and acquisitions in the corporate world, one means of interconnection among corporate interests is the selection of board of director members for a corporation. Such members are presumably selected because of their superior experience and understanding of the business and market working of any corporation. In theory, serving on the board does not necessarily imply deep technical understanding of manufacturing products. Due to their past successful experience, their serving on a board will assure economic financial success.

The interlocking process is well described by William Domhoff:

> The most objective starting point for grasping the full scope of the corporate community is in the interlocks created when a person sits on two or more corporate boards, because interlocks are the most visible and accessible of the ties among corporations. Since membership on a board of directors is public information, it is possible to use membership network analysis to make detailed studies of interlock patterns extending back into the early nineteenth century. The organizational network uncovered in these studies provides a rigorous research definition for the term corporate community: It consists of all those profit-seeking organizations connected into a single network by overlapping directors.
>
> However, it is very important not to overstate the actual importance of these interlocks. They are valuable for the dissemination of organizational innovations among corporations, they give the people who are members of several boards a very useful overview of the corporate community as a whole, they contribute to political cohesion, and they seem to have modest effects on some of the financial practices of the interlocked corporations. (Domhoff 2014, 16–17)

Interlocking board memberships were evident prior to the Great Recession of 2008–2012.

Under US antitrust law, interlocking directorates can be legal so long as the corporations involved do not directly compete. The website Investopedia said in 2017:

> Interlocking directorates were outlawed in specific instances where it gave a few board members control over an entire industry and allowed them to synchronize pricing changes, labor negotiations and so on. This does not prevent a board director from Company A from serving on the board of a Company B, which is a client of Company A. Although there are still many opportunities for collusion through interlocking

directorates, *recent trends in corporate governance have shifted much more power to the CEO.* Due to this shift, many CEOs have been able to appoint and dismiss board members as they please, as opposed to being influenced by them. (Interlocking Directorates website: https://www.investopedia.com/terms/i/interlocking-directorates.asp#ixzz502uXvJoX) (Emphasis added.)

Cooperative Supply Manufacturing

As mentioned above, with a description of the Ford CEO testifying before Congress in support of the government bailout of competitor General Motors, many oligopolies have developed control of supplier operations. There are many additional suggestions of this also provided above. As noted, dairy farming is one instance, and chicken produce is another.

An interesting example of global interaction was recently provided with one of the major corporations in the manufacture of commercial airliners, Boeing. The company recently assembled its new Dream Liner, Boeing 787, at a location in South Carolina. Paul Solma, in one of his "Making SEN$E" presentations on the PBS News Hour, held a conversation with Simon Johnson of the MIT Sloan School. From this, we learned that the new plane was not really built in the United States. A major part of the fuselage was built in Japan, the wings were also built in Japan, a smaller piece of the fuselage was built in Italy, the rudder was built in China, the stabilizer was built in Italy, and the landing gear was built in Great Britain, as were the Rolls-Royce engines. Only two positions were built in the United States: the cockpit was built in Kansas, and the tailpiece was built in South Carolina. Consequently, the plane was only *assembled* in the United States, while the majority of the parts came from global suppliers.

Boeing, of course, as the major world producer of commercial airliners, will be selling this product in many countries. However, the key point is that Boeing—a global, oligopolist corporation—operates in much the same worldwide fashion as automobile manufacturers like Ford and General Motors.[20] The large and

---

[20] The year 2019 has been a most difficult time for Boeing with its new 737 Max plane. Two crashes—one in 2018 and one in early 2019—killed all occupants and led to the plane being grounded in many countries.

highly controlling oligopolies are international in their use of influence in their buying and selling operations. One reason for this is that labor costs are significantly lower in countries other than the United States.

Another example is that of the Apple Corporation. Apple has a factory in a city in China, where they make iPhones. In this factory, the Chinese workers work a ten-hour day (6:00 a.m. to 6:00 p.m.) and a six-day week, or a total of sixty hours a week. They are paid $5.50 a day, which amounts to $33 per week. When you calculate the annual salary, it comes to $1,716. This suggests there is little incentive for Apple to close the China factory, build a new one somewhere in the US, and hire workers to work only a forty-hour week and be paid $15,000–$30,000 per year. One major incentive for the large-scale global spread of corporations (since the 1970s) has been the significant differential in global wages, where US and European wages are still much higher than those in other countries.

Violating the Federal Corrupt Practices Act

While much of the behavior involved in the actions by oligopoly corporations may be ethical or marginally unethical, there is significant corporate behavior that is illegal. One of the best examples of this is violation of the Foreign Corrupt Practices Act (FCPA). Information about these violations is provided by the Securities Exchange Commission.

The act was passed by Congress in 1977, as amended, 15 U.S.C. §§ 78dd-1, et seq. It was enacted for making it unlawful for classes of persons and entities to make payments to foreign government officials to assist in obtaining or retaining business.

> Specifically, the anti-bribery provisions of the FCPA prohibit the willful use of … any means of instrumentality of interstate commerce corruptly in furtherance of any offer, payment, promise to pay, or authorization of the payment of money … to any person, while knowing that all or a portion of such money or thing of value will be offered … to a foreign official to influence the foreign official in his or her official capacity, induce the foreign official to do … an act in violation of his or her lawful

duty, or to secure any improper advantage in order to assist in obtaining or retaining business for or with, or directing business to, any person. (https://www.justice.gov/criminal-fraud/foreign-corrupt-practices-act)

This act is regulated by the Securities and Exchange Commission, which provides case-by-case records of all charges of inappropriate use of bribery. Between the years 2000 and 2017, there have been 136 cases brought against both American and foreign corporations resulting in significant fines.

The year 2017 saw a total of $1 billion in corporate fines, while 2016 saw $3 billion in corporate fines. Fines to individuals in 2017 were $75,000 (for only one person, whose organization also paid a much larger fine). In 2016, $2.3 million was paid in individual fines. The top corporate fine in 2017 was $965 million. In 2016, there was also a top fine of $957 million. Also, in 2016, there were additional individual corporate fines of $765 million and $759 million.

The drop-in fines in 2017 were recently reported in the *New York Times* (November 4, 2018, p. 1 and 28–29) in an article headlined "Corporate Wrongdoers Get a Break under Trump." The summary findings were as follows:

> Comparing cases filed during the first 20 months of the Trump presidency with the final 20 months of the Obama administration, the review found:
>
> - a 62 percent drop in penalties imposed and illicit profits ordered returned by the SEC, to $1.9 billion under the Trump administration from $5 billion under the Obama administration;
> - a 72 percent decline in corporate penalties from the Justice Department's criminal prosecutions, to $3.93 billion from $14.15 billion and a similar percent drop in civil penalties against financial institutions, to $7.4 billion;
> - a lighter touch toward the banking industry, with the SEC ordering banks to pay $1.7 billion during the Obama period, nearly 4 times as much as in the Trump era, and Mr. Trump's Justice Department bringing 17 such cases, compared with 71.

Figure 3.5. Violations of the Foreign Corrupt Practices Act (FCPA), 2002–2017

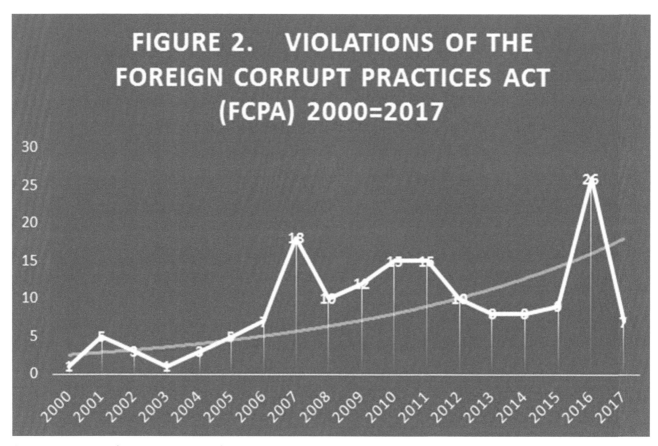

Source: Security Exchange Commission, https://www.sec.gov/spotlight/fcpa/fcpa-cases.shtml.

Table 3.5. Top corporations fined for violation of Foreign Corrupt Practices Act (FCPA), 2000–2017

42 best-known corporations among 136 cases in the 17 years

- Alcoa
- Anheuser-Bush
- Archer Daniels Midland Company
- AstraZeneca (UK)
- Avon Products
- Ball Corporation
- Biomet
- Braskan S.A. (Brazil)
- Bristol-Myers Squibb
- Cadbury
- Chevron
- Daimler Chrysler
- Diebold
- Dow Chemical Company
- Eli Lilly and Company
- General Cable Corporation
- General Electric
- GlaxoSmithKline (UK)
- Goodyear Tire & Rubber Company
- Halliburton
- Hewlett-Packard

- Hitachi
- IBM Corporation
- Ingersoll-Rand Company
- ITT Corporation
- Johnson & Johnson
- J.P. Morgan
- Monsanto Company
- Oracle
- Pfizer
- Pride International
- Ralph Lauren Corporation
- SciClone Pharmaceuticals
- Siemens
- Smith & Wesson
- Stryker CorporationTextron Inc.
- Tiva Pharmaceutical
- Tyco International
- Tyson Foods
- Volvo
- Westinghouse

Source: Securities Exchange Commission: https://www.sec.gov/spotlight/fcpa/fcpa-cases.shtml.

Conclusion

This chapter offers a broad view of today's global economic world. It is, however, unlike the previous chapter where I relied on the United Nations and their significant forecasts of urban population over the next fifteen to twenty-five years. It is important to consider the challenges that we face in this economic world. There is little forecasting of economic conditions over the long haul. At best, we can only speculate. For example, will the economic world move toward more broad holding companies such as Berkshire Hathaway? Clearly, the goal of mergers and acquisitions is not only to increase profits but also to increase power and control over more and more market segments. We are already seeing this to some extent in the rapid growth of power and scope of the very young firms of Apple, Google, and Facebook. Thus, we can imagine a world where oligopolies become larger in scope while smaller in number. If so, and if the UN forecasts for urbanization come true, what are the implications for urban planning in helping to solve Planet Earth's Tragedy of the Commons.

Thus, a major concern is the failure of the oligopolistic-corporatist economy to come to grips with global warming and environmental destruction. It is clear that today's economy is preeminent in contributing to planet Earth's Tragedy of the Commons. In addition, based on current corporate performance, we can presume we also face an uncontrolled future involving increasing inequality and significant neglect of basic human needs.

Dominant among these concerns is the extent to which the corporatist, oligopolistic economy involves a full range of greed, power, and control. In the next chapter, I will be discussing corporate control of government. Also, since the 1980s, there has been strong corporate control over the labor force. United States labor unions today are very small and primarily in local and state government, with some private unions operating in local construction. The labor unions that strongly contended with major companies in the 1930s have almost disappeared. Recently, the financial oligopoly has also been cutting back on retired workers' pension funds.

Inequality has become pronounced throughout the world. In the United States, current political practices virtually ignore the increasing inequality, both regionally and individually. The congressional tax policy act passed in December 2017 is seen by most economists as further magnifying inequality in the United States. As the leading economic nation, and given the dominant movement toward global, oligopolistic corporatism, inequality seems likely to remain a worldwide economic problem for 2030, the future year being forecast by United Nations for growing urban development, as laid out in chapter 2.

Recent books offer different long-term possibilities. This could include what we see today. On the one hand, we have the happy Scandinavian countries that seem to be doing well through an institutional framework of democratic socialism (*not* Stalinist communism). On the other hand, we see the rising Chinese state-dominated capitalism. Richard Wolff (2016) argues for the need of employees and labor unions taking over control of economic activity. That, of course, is not a forecast but rather expresses a normative Marxist-type plan for getting out of the mess we are now experiencing of severe global inequality.

There is a growing discipline known as ecological economics. These scholars have been led by Herman Daly and have focused on cap and trade, value-added taxes, and taxes on utilization of basic resources (Herman Daly 1996, 2014; Tim Jackson 2018).

Of course, any such forecasting does have to keep in mind the planetary boundaries described in chapter 2. Corporate interests over the long haul have created many adverse environmental effects. There is hope from the Paris Agreement of 2015 and the Katowice Conference in 2018 (except for the fact that the American government as of the time of this writing has withdrawn from the Paris and Katowice Agreements and has significantly retreated from environmental protection).[21]

Finally, how do the urban population trends set forth by the United Nations, as described in chapter 2, relate to the current trends in oligopolistic, corporatist economics? What are the future economic implications of a truly dominant urban population? Will the oligopolistic, corporatist dominance in economic behavior have significant effects on the urban development process in the coming years?

---

[21] The extent of diversion away from environmental protection was recently reported in the *New York Times* when EPA administrator Pruett left office. Published on July 9 was the article "76 Environmental Rules on the Way Out Under Trump."

These are critical questions for the planet Earth's Tragedy of the Commons. Obviously, some of the world's most powerful actors of today act according to their own self-interest and work contrary to the common good.

A key comment from the introduction of Wallerstein's book, *Does Capitalism Have a Future?* is useful in setting the stage for understanding potential future directions of today's corporatism:

> Capitalism, along with its creative destruction of older technologies and forms of production, has also been a source of inequality and environmental degradation. Deep capitalist crisis may be an opportunity to reorganize the planetary affairs of humanity in a way that promotes more social justice and a more livable planet. (Wallerstein et. al., page 4)

Yet another author is more pessimistic. In his recent book, *Extreme Cities*, Ashley Dawson describes in graphic terms what he sees as the future we face in a dominant global economy with increasing inequality.

> Around the globe, the hyperwealthy 1 percent are engaged in a feckless, hedonistic binge to end all binges, their systematic consumption obliterating the prospects of the poor, nature, and future generations. While they loot the planet, the rich live in well-protected penthouses and suburban garrisons, assiduously averting their eyes from the global majority, the swiftly deteriorating natural world, and the future they are so heedlessly obliterating. At present there is no way for future generations to interrupt the orgies of the rich, no way for the natural world to assert its rights, and slender chance for the victims of climate chaos to overthrow the tyranny of the 1 percent. (Dawson 2017, Kindle location 2073)

An equally cogent comment has been provided by the prominent economist Jeffrey Sachs:

> The system is indeed rigged for the big corporate interests such as the drug companies that set drug prices a thousand times the production cost. It's rigged for the large IT companies such as Apple Inc. that deploy egregious tax loopholes that enable them to park their funds overseas in tax-free offshore accounts. It's rigged for the hedge fund managers who take home hundreds of millions of dollars in pay and then face a top income tax rate of 20 percent, far below what other, vastly poorer Americans must pay. It's rigged for the investment bankers that deliberately cheated their clients and then walked away with a mere slap on the wrist, if that. (Sachs 2017, Kindle locations 1566–71)

Overall, it seems clear that the present world economy is not leaving us with a future that is in any way optimistic in terms of the Tragedy of the Commons for planet Earth. It is also difficult to comprehend how the oligopolistic-corporatist economy is going to help the urban planning process for the world. Another trend is quite dominant. Numerous authors see the dominance of today's corporatist, global economy as leading to the decline in efforts at pursuing and maintaining any form of democratic government. This is the key question in the next chapter. In addition, oligopolistic corporatism clearly poses significant problems for urban planning.

References

The references listed for this chapter were not necessarily cited in the chapter text. All, however, had a bearing on how I approached the writing of the text. I recommend them highly, as they provide the reader with a comprehensive view of what is happening in today's economic corporate world.

Brown, P. H. 2015. *How Real Estate Developers Think: Design, Profits, and Community.* Philadelphia: University of Pennsylvania Press.

Confessori, Nicholas. 2016. "How to hide $400 million." *New York Times* magazine, November 30, 2016.

Council of Economic Advisors Issue Brief. April 2016. *Benefits of Competition and Indicators of Market Power.* www.whitehouse.gov/sites/default/files/page/files/20160414_cea_competition_issue_brief.pdf.

Baker, Dean. 2016. *Rigged: How Globalization and the Rules of the Modern Economy Were Structured to Make the Rich Richer.* Washington, DC: Center for Economic and Policy Research.

Daly, Herman. 1996. *Beyond Growth: The Economics of Sustainable Development.* Boston: Beacon Press.

Daly, Herman. 2014. *From Uneconomic Growth to a Steady-State Economy.* Cheltenham, UK: Edward Elgar.

Dawson, A. 2017. *Extreme Cities: The Peril and Promise of Urban Life in the Age of Climate Change.* London: Verso Books.

Diefendorf, J. M. 2009. "Reconstructing Devastated Cities: Europe after World War II and New Orleans after Katrina." *Journal of Urban Design* 14, no. 3: 377–97.

Domhoff, G. William. 2014. *Who Rules America? The Triumph of the Corporate Rich.* 7th ed. New York: McGraw-Hill Education. Kindle edition.

Foer, Franklin. 2017. *World without Mind: The Existential Threat of Big Tech.* Penguin Press.

Galbraith, James. 2014. *The End of Normal: The Great Crisis and the Future Growth.* New York: Simon & Schuster.

Harvey, David. 2010. *The Enigma of Capital and the Crises of Capitalism.* New York: Oxford University Press.

Hill, Claire, and Richard W. Painter. 2017. *Better Bankers, Better Banks: Promoting Good Business through Contractual Commitment.* Chicago: University of Chicago Press.

Jackson, T. 2018. *Prosperity without Growth: Foundations for the Economy of Tomorrow.* 2nd ed. New York and London: Routledge.

Koblin, John. 2018. "Coming Soon to a Court Near You," *New York Sunday Times*, Business, pages 1 and 4.

Kuttner, R. 2018. *Can Democracy Survive Global Capitalism?* New York: W.W. Norton Company.

Lynn, Barry. 2010. *Cornered: The New Monopoly Capitalism and the Economics of Destruction.* Hoboken, NJ: John Wiley and Sons.

Nordhaus, William D. 2013. *The Climate Casino.* New Haven: Yale University Press.

Posner, E. A., and E. G. Weyl. 2018. *Radical Markets: Uprooting Capitalism and Democracy for a Just Society.* Princeton, NJ: Princeton University Press.

Ruth, Matthias. 2018. *Advanced Introduction to Ecological Economics.* Cheltenham, UK: Edward Elgar Publishing.

Sachs, J. D. 2017. *Building the New American Economy: Smart, Fair, and Sustainable.* New York: Columbia University Press.

Sampson, A. 1975. *The Seven Sisters: The Great Oil Companies and the World They Shaped.* New York: Viking.

Sassen, S. 2012. *Cities in a World Economy.* 4th ed. Los Angeles: Pine Forge Press (Sage).

Streeck, Wolfgang. 2016. *How Will Capitalism End? Essays on a Failing System.* Verso Books. Kindle edition.

Wallerstein, Immanual, Randall Collins, Michael Mann, Georgi Drerluguian, and Craig Calhoun. 2013. *Does Capitalism Have a Future?* Oxford: Oxford University Press.

Weiss, M. 1987. *The Rise of the Community Builders: the American Real Estate Industry and Urban Land Planning.* Washington, DC: BeardBooks.

Wolff, R. D. 2016. *Capitalism's Crisis Deepens: Essays on the Global Economic Meltdown.* Edited by M. L. Palmieri and D. Dallavalle. Chicago: Haymarket Books.

Wolin, Sheldon S. 2008. *Democracy Incorporated: Managed Democracy and the Specter of Inverted Totalitarianism.* Princeton, NJ: Princeton University Press. Kindle edition.

Wu, Tim. 2013. "The Oligopoly Problem," *New Yorker*, April 15.

Chapter 4

Corporate Control of Governance

Thomas Jefferson wrote in 1816, "I hope we shall … crush in [its] birth the aristocracy of our monied corporations which dare already to challenge our government … and bid defiance to the laws of our country."

In the late 1930s, Supreme Court Justice Louis Brandeis wrote, "We can have democracy in this country, or we can have great wealth concentrated in the hands of a few, but we cannot have both."

In virtually every part of the global planet, business and government coexist. In much of day-to-day life, the coexistence is accepted as normal with little dialogue. This, of course, varies according to which country one is living in. In authoritarian states, such as China or Russia, conflict with government is not the norm and is generally unacceptable and likely punishable. In such governments, the state rules business and corporate activity. In democratic governments, partnership and conflict are combined. In this chapter, major emphasis is on the United States, as this is the country with the largest oligopolistic, corporatist economy and where the antagonism between economics and governance is widely seen.

In the United States, there are only two parties competing for heading government. They tend to have differing arguments pertaining to the relationship of business and government. In other democratic governments, with parliamentarian rule, there may be more than two parties with quite varying attitudes toward the role of economic activity. What is important is the question of regulating the tendency toward monopoly power. Ecological economist Tim Jackson put it this way:

> As Adam Smith himself understood very clearly, some state intervention is needed to prevent or break up monopoly power. In fact, the bigger corporations become, the greater this need for the state. The efficient, free market which Smith proposed relied inherently on the fact that enterprises were relatively small, open to competition and responsive both to supplier pressure and to consumer demand. (Jackson 2017, 106)

Recent studies pertaining to corporate-government relations in other nations will be reviewed also. Finally, the chapter will review recent literature pertaining to prospects for future autocratic governance in place of democracy.

"The best government is the least government." "Keep government small." As a longtime US resident, I've heard Republicans saying this for more than seventy years. However, there is never any specific sense of what is the best *size* of government, nor has there been any specific definition of "least government." When I started voting (1952), the United States had slightly more than 152 million people. Now the nation has more than 330 million. Should the US government be the same size as it was in the 1950s? How does one determine the optimum size of government? What kind of measurement should we be making?

Republicans exalt the power of the free market and want the smallest possible government, with a tendency to leave the market alone—free of regulation. One has the sense the corporatist world would like the US to move back to when there was no such thing as a forty-hour week or a minimum pay standard. One also wonders if the corporatist world wants to take us back to the 1890s and early 1900s when worker fatalities and injuries were plentiful.[22] As noted in chapter 3, the Reagan administration in the 1980s started

---

[22] One most prominent case was the Triangle Shirtwaist Factory fire in 1911 where the owners had locked all doors, and the fire caused the deaths of 146 garment workers. The owners were determined not guilty. (Wikipedia). Today, those dangers still exist in poverty nations being exploited by capitalists. In 2012, a similar fire took place in Dhaka (in Bangladesh) where 117 people lost their lives, and more than two hundred were injured. This event also involved an apparel factory serving US consumers.

the process of strengthening capitalist relations over government and ignoring historic US antitrust law. As President Reagan once put it, "Government is not the solution to our problem; government is the problem."

Capitalism cannot exist without government (especially local, urban government). Capitalists and corporations (along with small, local business) cannot prosper without streets and highways, potable water, effective waste disposal, networked communications, policing to maintain social order, and educational and health systems that supply an educated, healthy workforce. Corporate firms in today's global economy even depend on government-supplied airports. Similarly, urban and national governments cannot exist without entrepreneurs providing employment for the population's labor force. Capitalism and urbanism are closely linked and interdependent (especially at the local, urban level).

Pressed to define "small" or "least government," it is unlikely that corporate leaders would want to lose any of these urban programs or infrastructure, although at the time of this writing, one of the country's two parties seems to be attempting to reduce both health care and education. Republicans see health care as a business, not as a primary human necessity. They see public education as inferior to private and charter schools. In addition, since the 1980s, major international corporations tend to rely primarily on significantly lower-cost laborers in poorer countries capable of routine, simple production tasks.

Today, government tends to be exploited by the corporatist oligopolies. When the nation has faced a social problem (poverty) or an opportunity (affordable housing), corporate behavior has been primarily obstructionism. This was especially true during the Obama administration, but it was also the pattern of behavior in the Clinton administration of the 1990s. In the early days of 2009, as the nation's first black president was moving into the White House, we heard from the southern Republican Senate leader that Obama was only going to serve one term, and there would be uniform Republican opposition to *whatever* he wanted to do. When the House was turned over to Republicans in 2010, there was little congressional action on any problem. From 2010 to 2016, there were forty separate House votes to repeal the Affordable Care Act (knowing President Obama would veto them) and no real effort to try to improve a major social responsibility for the nation. In 2013, Congress shut down the federal government for sixteen days, causing significant economic problems for the nation. In the Clinton administration, the Republican Party shut down the government twice.[23] In dealing with the important problems of global warming and environmental protection, obstructionism in the Donald Trump administration has come to the fore.

The Roberts Supreme Court and Its Benefits to Corporatism

In the United States, the Roberts Supreme Court, with *Citizens United* and other decisions, has legally brought corporate dominance into our allegedly democratic political processes. For more than one hundred years, corporate-government relations have varied. As corporations became dominant or corruptive, Congress historically passed restrictions. A diagram in an article by E. Rassweiler (2016) provides a good illustration of this.[24]

The overall effect of the *Citizens United* decision was clearly stated by Rassweiler:

> Not only did *Citizens United* allow corporations to spend unlimited amounts of money on political ads, but it also narrowed the legal definition of "corruption" to mean only outright bribery … It has become almost impossible to win court cases intended to stop what the average person would call corruption. The 2016 conservative victory at all levels of government has further dimmed prospects for reform in the near future. (p. 2)

The diagram illustrates a historical concern for inappropriate behavior in the election process. The *Citizens United* decision, however, eliminated any serious control on election funding. In effect, the funding role of corporations and wealthy individuals seeking to control government has been greatly enhanced.

---

[23] The modern term with the most government shutdowns was the Reagan administration that realized eight shutdowns over the eight years. These were always very short stoppages, with the longest lasting three days. The period of President Jimmy Carter's term of office had five shutdowns in his one-term, four-year presidency. Most recently, in 2018–2019, President Trump shut down the national government for over a month, the longest shutdown historically.

[24] Not included in the Rassweiler diagram was a court case in 1978 where the Supreme Court ruled that corporations have the same rights as natural-born citizens (*First National Bank of Boston v. Belotti*).

Figure 4.1

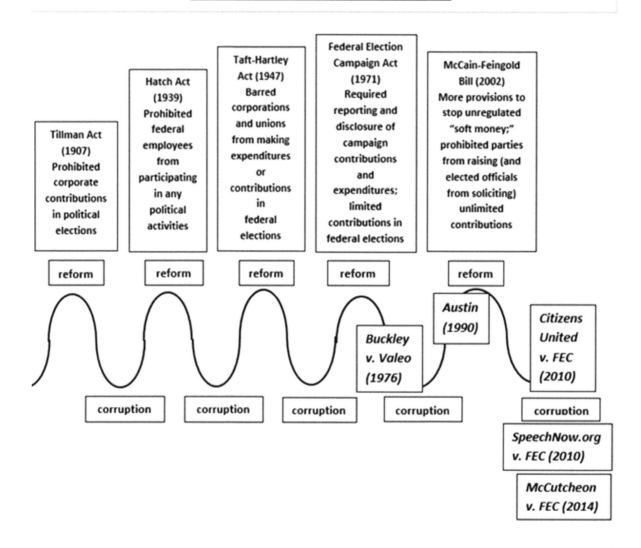

THE GENERAL CYCLICAL PATTERN OF CAMPAIGN FINANCE CORRUPTION AND REFORM
IN THE HISTORY OF UNITED STATES ELECTIONS

The effect of the *Citizens United* decision is well summarized by Jane Mayer in her book, *Dark Money*:

> On January 21, 2010, the Court announced its 5–4 decision in the Citizens United case, overturning a century of restrictions banning corporations and unions from spending all they wanted to elect candidates. The Court held that so long as businesses and unions didn't just hand their money to the candidates, which could be corrupt, but instead gave it to outside groups that were supporting or opposing the candidates and were technically independent of the campaigns, they could spend unlimited amounts to promote whatever candidates they chose. To reach the verdict, the Court accepted the argument that corporations had the same rights to free speech as citizens. (Mayer 2016, Kindle location 4322–27) (Refer also to footnote 26 above.)

Martin Gilens, in his recent book, *Affluence and Influence*, goes through sophisticated statistical analyses in the process of carrying out assessment of public polls concerning who most benefits from recent public policy decisions. While his methods are highly advanced, and his findings are complex, he provides one strong, conclusive statement:

> FEW WILL BE SURPRISED that the link between preferences and policies turns out to be stronger for higher-income Americans than for the poor. But the magnitude of this difference, and the inequality in representation that I find even between the affluent and the slightly less well-off, suggest that the political system is tilted very strongly in favor of those at the top of the income distribution. (Gilens 2012, Kindle location 1617)

The political dominance over the theoretically independent United States Supreme Court continues. Justice Scalia passed away in early 2016. President Obama selected a Supreme Court nominee; however, the predominantly Republican Senate refused to vote. When Donald Trump won the presidency, the Republican Senate approved Trump's nominee, and we are now seeing many Supreme Court 5–4 rulings that raise strong questions about gerrymandering and voting rights and President Trump's travel bans (Twitter by David Axelrod, reported in *New York Times*, June 26, 2018).

An immigration policy of Donald Trump attempting to limit immigration of people of Muslim religion was upheld by lower courts, but the United States Supreme Court approved this policy in June 2018. With the recent retirement of Associate Justice Anthony Kennedy, President Trump nominated another very conservative member of the court. After considerable controversy, Brett Kavanaugh was approved by the Senate, affirming a conservative court for many years.

Corporatism as a Lobbying Force

The American media pays close attention to partisan activity in the election process, including a high level of attention to corporate funding in election campaigns. However, corporations have a somewhat more active lobbying role in the *daily workings* of the legislative process (with very little media coverage). This role has many forms, but it takes place on a continual basis whenever a federal or state legislature is in session. At the national level, there is a widely known group of consulting lobbyists bearing the title of K Street firms. While technically each of us individually might visit Congress and lobby to have our proposal passed into law, high-priced lobbying firms primarily staffed by lawyers and hired by corporations to serve corporate interests carry out the bulk of lobbying activity. Additionally, retired members of the legislature are also hired to staff a lobbying firm.

Lobbying has been interpreted by court rulings as constitutionally protected free speech and a way to petition the government for the redress of grievances—two of the freedoms protected by the First Amendment of the Constitution. As noted by prominent economist George Stigler, lobbying can be described as "the capture of regulators by the regulated."

A quote from Lee Drutman quickly describes the diverse and effective ways in which lobbying influence the processes of public policymaking in the United States (2015, 1–2):

> Questions about the relationship of capitalism and democracy are as old as, well, both capitalism and democracy. What is new is that, in recent years, large corporations have achieved a pervasive position that is unprecedented in American political history. The most active companies now have upwards of 100 lobbyists representing them who are active on a similar number of different bills in a given session of Congress. They serve as *de facto* adjunct staff for congressional offices, drafting bills, providing testimony, and generally helping to move legislation forward. They provide policy expertise, helping stretched-too-thin staffers to get up to speed on a wide range of subjects and assisting administrative agencies in writing complex rules. They provide generous funding for think tanks and fill the intellectual environment of Washington with panel discussions and op-eds and subway advertisements. … They hire former congressional staffers and former members of Congress and former agency bureaucrats and former agency heads by the dozens to make sure they have a connection to every person who matters, as well as an insider's understanding on how the process works and how to work the process.

Data from the Center for Responsive Politics provides a specific look at the role of lobbying in the United States. The following table (table 4.1) indicates the total sums of money—at the billions level—involved in the lobbying process between 2008 and 2017. From the Center's website, table 4.2 identifies the major sectors of lobbying investment for 2016 and 2017.

In the decade between 2008 and 2017, a total of $25 billion was spent on lobbying, an average of almost $2.5 billion per year. Expenditures went up considerably in 2018, when the total lobbying spending amounted to $3.45 billion. Lobbying is clearly a most significant part of the interactive relationship between business and government.

Some of the top firms' lobbying expenditures in the first quarter of 2017 were Google at $3.5 million, Chevron at $3.3 million, Facebook at $3.2 million, Teva Pharmaceuticals at $2.7 million, National Rifle Association at $2.2 million, and Apple at $1.4 million. During 2018, the US Chamber of Commerce was the top spender at nearly $95 million. They were followed by the National Association of Realtors ($73 million) and the pharmacy group Pharmaceutical Research and Manufacturers of America (PhRMA), spending $28 million in 2018. The spending of individual pharmacies included Pfizer ($11.3 million), Johnson & Johnson ($6.6 million), and AbbVie ($6.1 million) (https://www.opensecrets.org/news/2019/01/lobbying-spending-reaches-3-4-billion-in-18/).

Table 4.1. Total lobbying expenditures, 2008–2017

Source: Center for Responsive Politics, https://www.opensecrets.org/lobby/incdec.php.

Total Spent	Year	Number of Lobbyists
$2,467,646,129	2017	11,078
$2,381,165,809	2016	10,945
$2,420,601,829	2015	11,254
$2,434,346,671	2014	11,553
$2,406,842,056	2013	11,788
$2,472,880,181	2012	11,916
$2,477,241,015	2011	12,239
$2,645,131,105	2010	12,605
$2,532,984,616	2009	13,319
$2,490,331,498	2008	13,708

Table 4.2. Sectors of lobbying investment for 2016–2017

Source: Center for Responsive Politics, https://www.opensecrets.org/lobby/incdec.php.

Sectors	2016 3rd Quarter	2017 3rd Quarter	Difference	% Change
Health	$124,328,387	$127,937,821	$3,609,434	2.9%
Finance, insurance, and real estate	$128,121,228	$119,383,356	$-8,737,872	-6.8%
Communications/electronics	$90,356,000	$98,840,123	$8,484,123	9.4%
Energy and natural resources	$70,624,607	$72,282,389	$1,657,782	2.3%
Transportation	$55,150,944	$58,290,741	$3,139,797	5.7%
Ideological/single-issue	$32,294,622	$34,269,679	$1,975,057	6.1%
Agribusiness	$29,270,464	$30,879,725	$1,609,261	5.5%
Defense	$29,285,728	$29,012,508	$-273,220	-0.9%
Construction	$12,527,165	$14,917,241	$2,390076	19.1%
Labor	$12,516,507	$11,598,046	$-918,461	-7.3%
Lawyers and lobbyists	$5,074,328	$5,107,531	$33,203	0.7%
Other	$47,869,903	$49,074,081	$1,204,170	2.5%
Miscellaneous business	$128,121,228	$119,383,356	$-,737,872	-6.8%

The Underground Funding Stream

Jane Mayer, in *Dark Money* (2016), describes what she labeled the Underground Funding Stream leading to the power development of corporations and very wealthy individuals. The creation of this funding stream is discussed in detail in the first part of her book, where the predominant message is that the key leaders of corporate dominance over governance lies with people who primarily inherited large financial wealth—people who already had a lot money at birth. These included the Koch brothers, Richard Mellon Scaife, John Olin, the Bradley brothers, Sheldon Adelson, and others.

She describes a three-phase takeover of American politics:

> The first phase required an "investment" in intellectuals whose ideas would serve as the "raw products." The second required an investment in think tanks that would turn the ideas into marketable policies. And the third phase required the subsidization of "citizens" groups that would, along with "special interests," pressure elected officials to implement the policies. It was in essence a libertarian production line, waiting only to be bought, assembled, and switched on. (Mayer 2016, Kindle location 2708)

This funding stream has been going on for several years. The first part, investment in intellectuals, found multimillionaires taking on the enlistment of intellectuals by giving large sums of money to top universities. In the past, wealth holders had strong feelings that universities were promoting largely leftist thinking, so the funds given to the universities had conditions providing for (or requiring) market-oriented intellectuals. The second phase is marked by the creation of dominant nonprofit foundation groups such as the Cato Institute, the American Heritage Foundation, Americans for Prosperity Foundation, Freedom Works, the Hoover Institution, the Bradley Foundation, and The John M. Olin Foundation (to name a few). To complete this, as noted above, is the strong placing of money into election campaigns.

It should also be noted that the corporatist, oligopolistic regime has significantly taken control of labor as well as government. As is well known, labor unions have almost disappeared, particularly in the corporate area. Labor unions continue to exist, but they are predominantly local in their nature; they are found in state and local government and are also found in local construction firms. People working in the top-level capitalist realm are very much under control of corporate dominance.

In sum, through control of election campaigns, ongoing lobbying, millionaire-supported philanthropic entities (Cato Institute, etc.), and pushing universities to enlist right-leaning intellectuals, the wealthy have considerable influence over the United States government, together with more than half of the nation's state governments (aided by the American Legislative Exchange Council—ALEC). The rise of the corporatist, oligopolistic economy seriously raises the question: is the US today really a democratic nation?

Corporate Avoidance of Taxes

United States tax laws contain many loopholes—thanks to corporate influence on elections and lobbying. As a result, many of the nation's largest corporations pay either zero taxes or taxes well below the so-called limit in the tax law. Before December 2017, corporations were supposed to pay 35 percent of their profits in federal taxes (as well as state and local taxes). In December 2017, the United States Congress passed a new tax law that lowered the corporate tax rate to 21 percent. However, studies have shown that during the time corporations were supposed to pay 35 percent, the actual average of corporate tax payment was around 21.2 percent. In addition, there were numerous large corporations whose actual tax bill was zero. The most prominent corporation paying zero taxes was General Electric.

A study by the Institute on Taxation and Economic Policy was carried out analyzing 258 corporations for the period 2008 to 2015. Some of the key findings include the following:

- As a group, the 258 corporations paid an effective federal income tax rate of 21.2 percent over the eight-year period, slightly over half the statutory 35 percent tax rate.
- Eighteen of the corporations, including General Electric, International Paper, Priceline.com and PG&E, paid *no federal income tax at all over the eight-year period*. A fifth of the corporations (48) paid an effective tax rate of less than 10 percent over that period.

- Of those corporations in our sample with significant offshore profits, more than half paid higher corporate tax rates to foreign governments where they operate than they paid in the United States on their U.S. profits.
- One hundred of the 258 companies (39 percent of them) paid zero or less in federal income taxes in at least one year from 2008 to 2015.
- Five companies—AT&T, Wells Fargo, J.P. Morgan Chase, Verizon, and IBM—enjoyed more than $130 billion in tax breaks during the eight-year period. (https://itep.org/the-35-percent-corporate-tax-myth/) (Emphasis added.)

One of the major loopholes in tax law is that American multinational corporations can "indefinitely defer" US taxes on their *offshore* profits. In effect, this loophole encourages global corporations to shift both jobs and profits to other countries. The ITEP Report sums it up: "The tax laws were not enacted in a vacuum; they were adopted in response to relentless corporate lobbying, threats and campaign support."

Table 4.3. Summary of eight-year tax rates: 258 companies, 2008–2015

Source: Institute on Taxation and Economic Policy, https://itep.org/the-35-percent-corporate-tax-myth/.

Effective Tax Rate Group	Number of Companies	Percent of Companies	2008–2015 $Billion		
			Profits	Tax	Avg. Rate
Less than 17.5%	83	32%	$1,274.2	$107.5	8.4%
17.5 to 30%	109	42%	1,267.2	393.7	24.2
More than 30%	66	26%	909.2	305.7	33.6
All 258 Firms	258	100%	3,810.6	806.9	21.2%

The Institute on Taxation and Economic Policy, in a web page report in April 2019, indicated that corporations under the 2017 tax law have increased their getaway from taxation. As reported by the institute:

> An in-depth analysis of Fortune 500 companies' financial filings finds that at least 60 of the nation's biggest corporations didn't pay a dime in federal income taxes in 2018 on a collective $79 billion in profits, the Institute on Taxation and Economic Policy said today. (https://itep.org/60-fortune-500-companies-avoided-all-federal-income-tax-in-2018-under-new-tax-law/)

Corporate Power Internationally

Corporate power internationally is also evident, although in a world of hundreds of countries, there is considerable variation. Nations that are poor actively encourage corporations to locate within their borders. These countries often have low labor costs and tax rates for corporations as an incentive to encourage corporate location. Ireland has been a prominent example. Many corporations in the United States have relocated their firm headquarters to Ireland for that reason.

Perhaps a most outstanding example was relocation of the headquarters of Medtronic Corporation in January 2015. It was accompanied by the merger and acquisition of a competitor, Covidien, which was also headquartered in Dublin at that time (Covidien originally was in Massachusetts, USA, and moved to Dublin in 2007). Not only were taxes avoided, but also avoided were any possible antitrust restrictions on the merger.

For another example, the *Washington Post* reported on the Apple Corporation on September 9, 2016:

> In 2013, for instance, Tim Cook, Apple's chief executive, was called before a Senate panel to explain the tech giant's tax strategies. A Senate investigation had concluded that Apple used a "complex web" of offshore entities to shield at least $74 billion in profits from U.S. tax laws between 2009 and 2012. The company had a special arrangement with Irish authorities to pay little to no taxes on profit housed in its subsidiaries, the report found.

From Apple's annual report to the United States government, Apple owns or rents buildings throughout Europe, China, Singapore, and Japan. In 2014, the company owned a manufacturing facility in Cork, Ireland.

More examples can be found on the website of CNBC describing ten US companies that have moved to other countries. (https://www.cnbc.com/2016/04/21/10-iconic-us-companies-that-have-moved-headquarters-abroad.html?slide=12):

1. Burger King, following its acquisition of Tim Hortons, moved to Canada, saving as much as $275 million in taxes (this is part of 3G Capital, discussed in chapter 3).
2. Budweiser was bought out in 2008 by InBev and thus is part of the beer conglomerate based in Belgium (also part of 3G Capital).
3. Medtronic moved to Ireland in 2014 when it bought Covidien for $42.9 billion.
4. Purina pet food company merged with Nestlé in 2001 and is now headquartered in Switzerland.
5. McDermott, a New Orleans construction company in the 1980s, shifted its headquarters to Panama (this was ruled legal by US courts in 1987).
6. Seagate Technology, a computer hard drive manufacturer, moved from Cupertino, California, to Ireland in 2010 (at one point, the company had previously been headquartered in the Cayman Islands).
7. In 1961, UK's Unilever purchased Good Humor Ice Cream Bar. Unilever also oversees Ben & Jerry's, Breyers, Magnum, Klondike, and other companies.
8. Frigidaire was once sold to General Motors, was then bought by Consolidated Industries, and finally was taken over by Sweden's Electrolux, so the American company has its global headquarters overseas.
9. Actavis/Allergan moved from New Jersey to Dublin, Ireland, in 2013.
10. Lucky Strike cigarettes were bought in the 1990s by British American tobacco so is now headquartered in England and is a popular, growing brand in Europe.

One of the most outstanding examples of corporate power lies in the ability to escape taxation altogether in foreign international business dealings. A chapter in Robert Kuttner's recent book provides strong documentation of foreign tax haven countries. The history goes far back, indicating that Switzerland has been a tax-free haven since the early twentieth century. Another place that has received some publicity is the Cayman Islands. Kuttner summarizes the current situation as follows:

> The Congressional Research Service found that US - based multinational corporations booked 43 percent of their foreign earnings in five tax haven countries: Bermuda, Ireland, Luxembourg, the Netherlands, and Switzerland. Yet only 4 percent of these companies' foreign workforces were actually based in those countries. All told, Fortune 500 corporations hold about $ 2.5 trillion in profits booked outside the US purely for tax avoidance purposes. (Kuttner 2018, chapter 9)

Additionally, from the website of the Institution on Taxation and Economic Policy: "60 Profitable Fortune 500 Companies Avoided All Federal Income Taxes in 2018." (after the passage of the Tax law in 2017) (https://itep.org/notadime/)

From a very different part of the world, a growing global economic force is found in state-owned transnational enterprises (TSOE), particularly in the nations of China and Russia. Since the Great Recession in 2008, the economic growth in China moves beyond many of the economic recovering "democratic" governments of Europe and other regions. Today, China is second only to the United States in economic growth. A recent report in the *New Yorker* magazine makes the following note:

> In 2000, the U.S. accounted for thirty-one percent of the global economy, and China accounted for four percent. Today, the U.S.'s share is twenty-four percent and China's fifteen percent. If its economy surpasses America's in size, as experts predict, it will be the first time in more than a century that the world's largest economy belongs to a non-democratic country. At that point, China will play a larger role in shaping, or thwarting, values such as competitive elections, freedom of expression and an open Internet. (Osnos 2018, 7)[25]

---

[25] Recently (March 2018), President Xi Jinping of China was voted to serve a lifetime of rule.

As noted in the previous chapter, China has the top banking corporations in the world and leads in petroleum resources. China also invests substantially in land in other countries, particularly in Africa, where they are investing in the pursuit of oil and uranium. In effect, state-owned transnational enterprises (TSOE) are demonstrating equal or better economic growth than private transnational enterprises in traditional developed nations.[26] The current US president has recognized the dominance of China's economic growth and has opened a trade war that seems to recognize fear of possible impact of TSOE on the US economy.

The Decline of Democracy

Many authors see the dominance of the corporatist economy as leading to the decline in efforts at pursuing and maintaining a democratic government. I had an experience many years ago as an elected government official. It was in a small town in Massachusetts with a population of about 3,500 people. This was a New England town meeting government and was the closest thing I have ever experienced to an actual democracy. As a nation of 350 million people, we are very distant from being a democracy; our individual voices have little volume in the pursuit of political processes and projects. Economic inequality in the United States is intertwined with political inequality. The wealthy in effect have managed control of their environment—not simply economic control but political control as well.[27]

A recent book by Stephen Levitsky, *How Democracies Die*, provides a useful history of how democracy has been eliminated by authoritarian leaders, going back to Hitler in the 1930s. As Levitsky points out,

---

[26] A comprehensive study of illegal money handling worldwide is also available on the internet. Referred to as the "Panama Papers," key factors can be found on https://www.icij.org/investigations/panama-papers/.

[27] The original design of the Constitution did not see every voter as equal. This was evident in the 2016 election where the winner got the most electoral votes, but the loser actually had 3.5 million *more* individual votes. This is also evident in the makeup of the Senate. Every state has two senators; however, California has 39.5 million people, New York has 19.5 million people, and Wyoming has 550,000. Each Wyoming senator has equal power to that of each California and each New York senator. Every Wyoming constituent, in effect, is seventy-two times more powerful than a California constituent and thirty-five times more powerful than a New York constituent.

however, not only generals and authoritarians can take away a democracy. Given an international world, this can also take place with the help of other governments. When Allende won the electoral vote for president of Chile, other governments, including the United States government, suspected that he was a communist. Consequently, with international help, he was assassinated and overthrown, and Pinochet ruled as the dictator of Chile for many years. In another Latin American nation, Venezuela, Hugo Chavez became president in a democratic election. He won in 2002 and in 2006, but in his term, he became more and more authoritarian. After his death, his successor, Nicholas Maduro, became even more authoritarian, so that today Venezuela has no relationship to democracy. Levitsky notes:

> Since the end of the Cold War, most democratic breakdowns have been caused not by generals and soldiers but by elected governments themselves … elected leaders have subverted democratic institutions in Georgia, Hungary, Nicaragua, Peru, the Philippines, Poland, Russia, Sri Lanka, Turkey, and Ukraine. Democratic backsliding today begins at the ballot box. (Levitsky 2017, 5)[28]

Democratic countries having significant share of the Fortune 500 corporations are experiencing the decline of democracy by way of the power and resources of the corporatist, oligopolistic economy. With the arrival of the Great Recession in 2009, public awareness of the great inequality was highlighted in the Occupy Wall Street demonstration in New York in the fall of 2011. This represented a significant public reaction to a high level of income inequality. However, at this writing, income inequality is much higher today than it was in 2011. In 2016, the top 1 percent took home more than 20 percent of all US income. The bottom 50 percent went from capturing over 20 percent of national income for much of the 1970s to earning barely 12 percent in 2016 (http://money.cnn.com/2016/12/22/news/economy/us-inequality-worse/index.html).

I close with quotes from two prominent European economists. The first is from Wolfgang Merkel in his publication, "Is Capitalism Compatible with Democracy?":

---

[28] In October 2018, Brazil could be added to the list of new authoritarian governments with the election of Jair Bolsanaro, who wants to convert more of the Amazon forest into farmland.

91

Among the consequences for democracy, are four: 1) asymmetric political participation – the exclusion of the lower classes from the political process – caused by rising inequality and poverty; 2) the impossibility in open polities for democratic politics to stem the rise in economic inequality; 3) the pressures in financialized national economies on governments to turn their countries into 'market-conforming democracies;' and 4) the transfer of decision-making powers under globalization towards the executives, at the expense of parliaments. (Merkel 2014, 109–128)

My second German economist is Wolfgang Streep from his book, *How Will Capitalism End? Essays on a Failing System*. His discussion focuses on what he terms as the "Hayekian dictatorship of the market":[29]

Hayekian democracy serves the function of making a capitalist market society appear to be 'the people's choice' even though it has long been removed from democratic control. What I refer to as a technocratic-authoritarian market dictatorship is a political-economic regime that delegates decisions on the distribution of people's life chances to the 'free play' of market forces or, which is the same, concentrates them in the hands of executive agencies that supposedly command the technical knowledge necessary to organize such markets so that they perform best. (Streep 2016, Kindle location 3317)

---

[29] A leading theorist of modern right-wing political movements was the Austrian economist Friedrich Hayek, perhaps best noted for his book *The Road to Serfdom*, considered a "penetrating analysis of the interdependence of economic, social and institutional phenomena" (Wikipedia).

Conclusion

When we combine the United Nations' picture of world urban populations taking place on a planet of corporate, oligopolistic dominance versus authoritarian dominance and the decline of democratic governments, all occurring with continuing use and abuse of planet Earth's global natural facilities (water, ozone, nitrogen, phosphorus, etc.), one might have a negative outlook on the future. As China's president was quoted saying at Davos in 2017, "Today, we also live in a world of contradictions" (Mishra 2018, 44).

A wonderful summary of today's dominance of capitalism has been provided by Ian Gough:

> I take 'actually existing neoliberalism' to be a distinct phase of capitalism since around 1980. It embraces a dominant set of ideas and of practices. It's defining ideas included a belief in the superiority of markets and a denigration of much government and collective action. It's defining characteristics include a new international division of labor, the global spread of production networks, trade and financial flows, the dominance of finance, rising profit shares and widening inequalities within countries. (Gough 2017, 11)

Another equal concern is the role of technology today, as it has evolved in the last quarter century. These technologies have not only influenced the way we live our lives, but they have also made significant changes in the character of our economic, social, and political institutions. Technology has also played a key role in changing the nature of the global labor force. This, then, is the critical concern of the next chapter. It should also be noted that while technology may have emerged in the 1980s and 1990s by single innovators such as Bill Gates or Mark Zukerman, today, innovation and creativity is dominated by the corporatist world. In psychological terms, where greed dominated in the late 1980s, power and control are dominant today.

One thing for certain is the question, What types and forms of urban development can we envision over the next fifteen to twenty years under these intimidating economic and political circumstances? With corporate dominance over labor unions, along with dominance over national and international governments, is there a role for local government? With the United Nations' forecast of urban population, can a local form of government—an urban government, or even a network of urban governments—work to counter economic or authoritarian domination and serve the lifelong education, health, and economic needs of urban dwellers? Some authors have addressed this question and will be discussed in our final chapter.

In our overview of the planet Earth's Tragedy of the Commons, it is clear, as noted, that many people are indeed pursuing their own self-interest, and they are succeeding by dominating institutions of production and sales while diminishing governance. It is thereby clear that any institutional framework that might seek to diminish or eliminate the Tragedy of the Commons is becoming weaker as time goes by. A foundational institutional framework for supporting social responsibility is seriously declining. A needed institutional structure is well described in a quote from Dani Roderik, Professor of International Political Economy at Harvard University:

> In my own work, I have always emphasized the need for a mixed economy, *in which the government and markets reinforce each other.* (my emphasis)

References

Center for Responsive Politics. https://www.opensecrets.org/lobby/incdec.php.

Drutman, L. 2015. *The Business of America Is Lobbying: How Corporations Became Politicized and Politics Became More Corporate*. New York: Oxford University Press.

Domhoff, G. W. 2014. *Who Rules America? The Triumph of the Corporate Rich*. New York: McGraw-Hill Education.

Gelles, D. 2013. "New Corporate Tax Shelter: A Merger Abroad." *New York Times*, October 18, 2013.

Gilens, M. 2012. *Affluence and Influence: Economic Inequality and Political Power in America*. Princeton, NJ: Princeton University Press and the Russell Sage Foundation.

Grayling, A. C. 2017. *Democracy and Its Crisis*. Oneworld.

Institute on Taxation and Economic Policy. 2017. "The 35% Corporate Tax Myth." https://itep.org/the-35-percent-corporate-tax-myth/.

Jackson, T. 2018. *Prosperity without Growth: Foundations for the Economy of Tomorrow*. 2nd ed. New York and London: Routledge.

Kurlantzick, J. 2016. *State Capitalism: How the Return of Statism Is Transforming the World*. New York: Oxford University Press.

Kurlantzick, J. 2013. *Democracy in Retreat: The Revolt of the Middle Class and the Worldwide Decline of Representative Government*. New Haven, CT: Yale University Press.

Kuttner, R. 2018. *Can Democracy Survive Global Capitalism?* New York: W.W. Norton Company.

Levitsky, S., and D. Ziblatt. 2018. *How Democracies Die*. New York: Crown Publishing Group.

Luckerson, V. 2015. "Here's How Much Pfizer Could Save in Taxes after Allergan Merger." *Time* magazine (November 23, 2015).

Mayer, Jane. 2016. *Dark Money: The Hidden History of the Billionaires behind the Rise of the Radical Right*. New York: Doubleday.

McBride, W. 2014. "Another U.S. Company Moves to Ireland for Tax Reasons." The Tax Foundation. https://taxfoundation.org/another-us-company-moves-ireland-tax-reasons.

Merkel, W. 2014. "Is Capitalism Compatible with Democracy?" *Zeitschrift für Vergleichende Politikwissenschaft* 8, no. 2: 109–128.

Mishra, P. 2018. "Great Walls," *New York Times* magazine (February 11, 2018): 44–49.

OECD. 2016. *Financing Democracy: Funding of Political Parties and Election Campaigns and the Risk of Policy Capture.* OECD public governance reviews, OECD publishing, Paris.

http://dx.doi.org/10.1787/9789264249455-en.

Osnos, E. 2018. "Making China Great Again." *New Yorker.* https://www.newyorker.com/magazine/2018/01/08/making-china=great-again.

Rassweiler, E. 2017. *Corporate Control of Elections: Citizens United V. Federal Election Commission (2010)* and Related Decisions: The History and Consequences. https://corporatecontrolofelections.com/.

Streeck, Wolfgang. 2016. *How Will Capitalism End? Essays on a Failing System.* Verso Books. Kindle edition.

Chapter 5

The Role of Technology

Given the urban population trends forecasted by the United Nations, and the economic and political circumstances laid out in chapters 3 and 4, the next trends to explore are those of technology. Most of us are aware of these. As of this writing, I have had a cell phone for at least five years, and I recently bought a new one and discovered a few new features that are very useful. I watch cable television and videos from YouTube, Netflix, and Hulu. I have been driving a hybrid car for many years. We all live in this twenty-first-century technological world.

At this stage in life, I have many memories of past, momentous increases in technology. As a child, I attended the 1939 New York World's Fair, where I saw the first television set to be on public display. I had a relative that worked for RCA and thus got to watch at his home the very first *color* television show—*The Dinah Shore Show*—on a Sunday evening. Working for the city of Boston, I worked with one of the original computers by the Remington-Rand Corporation. It filled an entire room in the city hall basement. There was no software but a pegboard designed for me to give the computer specific instructions. Later, I worked with one of the original IBM computers as well (occupying only one quarter of a room). I bought the very first laptop computer originally marketed by RadioShack.

The city planning profession has benefitted from the new technologies. Community participation in planning is aided by social communication. Planners' technical skills have also been increased through data collection, mapping software, and more advanced analytical and statistical techniques. However, urban planning, as yet, has not given close attention to how new technology may impact urban labor forces, which may then impact markets for housing and urban services. Can new technologies have influence in future urban living? Can new technologies create urbanity that avoids or stops the Tragedy of the Commons?

Accordingly, in this chapter, technological trends are explored not in purely technological terms but in economic, social, and urban planning terms. Technology in the twenty-first century has had a marked impact on how we interact with one another, how we need to educate ourselves, and how the kinds of jobs available have significantly changed. The chapter is organized to explore the implications for the future of trends in artificial intelligence, robotic production, energy, retail marketing, transportation, agriculture, and military capability.

Overall, technological research and sales activity today is internationally widespread. On the web, you can find periodic inventories of new inventions and activities. MIT provides an annual upgrade on new technology, as does the magazine *Popular Mechanics.* The activities are generally described as threefold: (1) artificial intelligence, (2) robotics, and (3) health research and applications. It should be kept in mind that these three are very much interrelated. These activities may be very deep in detail, and if they are, they are not widely understood by the general public. Others may get a high level of public attention; for example, the Mall of America, the nation's largest retail and recreation mall, now has human-looking robots that will help guide you to whatever store, restaurant, or recreational activity you want to find. You can also buy a robot that will clean your home or mow your lawn. I have grandchildren with toy drone aircraft (which helps amuse and educate them when they are not engaged in interstate TV games).

This activity is by no means limited to the United States. In fact, China and India are the two leading nations in artificial technology usage. These two countries lead in the distribution of cell phones among their populations, including availability to low-income people. In the United States, the role of corporations is clearly dominant. Historically, however, leading corporations today were not really in existence in the year 2000: Google, Facebook, and Amazon, along with Verizon and Comcast. The emergence of this brand-new corporate oligopoly has been fast, predominately in the last twenty years.

Telecommunications and Artificial Intelligence

Imagine you were the CEO of a corporation back in the 1970s, when economic globalization really began. Say, for example, the corporation you owned was headquartered in Pittsburgh, and you wanted to merge with a business in Germany. This would entail many visits to Germany at considerable direct, out-of-pocket cost, including your airfare, hotel bills, meals, and local transportation. Today, you can use the Internet, Skype, and your cell phone and create your business in Germany with virtually no out-of-pocket travel cost. Also, back in the 1970s, acquiring the capital to purchase the new facility meant substantial money from your wallet or your bank, whereas today, arrangements are made electronically. All the money transactions involved are digitized, no matter what national currencies are involved. As pointed out by Castells (2010) and Sassen (2012), global, corporate economics have created significant interlocking *networks* aided, abetted, and dominated by urban telecommunications infrastructure. In fact, as I suggested in my cartoon in chapter 3 (figure 3.4), through telecommunications, the banking and monetary services of a global economy dominate nearly all aspects of today's economic, corporatist activity.

Social communications have clearly become important and have changed the way we live in many ways—economically, socially, and politically. The cell phone has revolutionized our abilities to communicate by voice and text messages. We can watch videos through our iPads or cell phones without depending on local or cable TV. With communication skills today, we can function in all aspects of life with little reliance on the traditional paper bills and metal coins. We can electronically borrow money, loan it, launder it, and hide it. We can do this all sitting in our office or even at home.

Recent advances in telecommunications and artificial intelligence include 3-D printing,[30] neural networks (involving Google leadership), technology to enhance privacy, and improved facial-recognition technology, along with other applications. The *Washington Post* reported the following in January 2016:

> There have been major advances in "deep learning" neural networks, which learn by
> ingesting large amounts of data: IBM has taught its A.I. system, 'Watson,' everything

---

[30] 3-D printing has truly advanced to the point of building prefabricated buildings. On the down side, we now have 3-D printing that gives us guns.

from cooking, to finance, to medicine and Facebook. Google and Microsoft have made great strides in face recognition and human-like speech systems. A.I.-based face recognition, for example, has almost reached human capability. And IBM 'Watson' can diagnose certain cancers better than any human doctor can.

There have also been negative aspects of contemporary technological communication development. The one receiving the greatest publicity today is the evidence of Russian interference in the 2016 presidential campaign in the United States. This has also exposed the broad-scale invasion of privacy employed by a UK firm called Cambridge Analytica delving into the files of Facebook. As a cell phone user, I have become seriously and fully aware of robocalls.

Overall, social communications have created great advantages but also serious difficulties, especially in the invasion of privacy.

Artificial Intelligence and Urban Planning

A new project in Toronto, called Quayside, is hoping to change the patterns of urban design by rethinking an urban neighborhood from the ground up and rebuilding it around the latest digital technologies. The project involves an abandoned waterfront industrial area. The newly planned neighborhood aims to be the first place to successfully integrate modern urban design with state-of-the-art digital technology. The key orientation is that using the ideas of smart cities, one can make urban areas more affordable, livable, and environmentally friendly. This project was first announced in October 2017, and construction is expected to begin in 2019.

A business firm based in New York City, Alphabet's Sidewalk Labs, is collaborating with the Canadian government on the project. One key goal is to base decisions about design, policy, and technology on information from an extensive network of sensors that gather detailed and deep data on everything from air quality to noise levels to people's activities. The plan calls for all vehicles to be autonomous and shared. Alphabet's Sidewalk Labs indicates it will open access to the software and systems it is creating so others can build services on top of them, similar to the process of building apps for mobile phones.

Alphabet's Sidewalk Labs wants to transform the area into one of the world's most innovative city neighborhoods. Elizabeth Woyke, of MIT, describes the goals:

> It will, in the company's vision, be a place where driverless shuttle buses replace private cars; traffic lights track the flow of pedestrians, bicyclists, and vehicles; robots transport mail and garbage via underground tunnels; and modular buildings can be expanded to accommodate growing companies and families. (Source: https://www.technologyreview.com/s/610249/a-smarter-smart-city/)

Uncertainties suggest the urban plan is not yet comprehensive. Toronto is overall economically vibrant and prosperous. It is not clear, however, that the project's housing would be both economically and geographically desirable. It is also not clear how its transport technologies or its garbage robots will connect with the rest of the city. It does look like the project is attractive and technologically modern and new. However, in chapter 7, I suggest the need for much broader, more interdisciplinary work in urban planning.

Robotic Production

Robotic production has been underway for many years. In the process, it has made many alterations to the character of employment. Pictures of an automobile factory in the 1950s and 1960s show hundreds of workers along assembly lines doing specific small-scale hand tasks. These small, individual tasks ultimately produced parts that were then assembled by more hand workers. The factories were crowded, and many people had jobs. Employment grew as car sales grew in the 1950s. The jobs, however, did not require high levels of skill, by today's standards, although the growth of sales tended to mean more jobs and rising pay (given the existence of strong labor unions at the time).

However, car manufacturers, along with other manufacturers, began to think of and develop ways in which tasks could be accomplished by machines rather than people. This happened as other forms of manufacturing began to seek out lower-paying wages in foreign countries for low and moderately skilled workers (such as apparel and electronics). However, automobiles and other heavy machinery manufacturing began to develop what today is called robotics.

A recent report of McKinsey & Company provides indications of what this change in manufacturing technique means today. In a 2017 report, they indicated that about half of current work activities are technically automatable by adapting existent technologies. The report also indicates that 60 percent of current occupations have more than 30 percent of work activities that could be automatable. The report indicates that by 2030, as many as four hundred million employees could be displaced by automation. It also states that a sizable extent of workers would have to change their skills and operations to maintain employment. The report estimates that up to 30 percent of the hours worked globally could be automated by 2030, depending on the speed of adoption.

The McKinsey Report concludes with the following:

> When we look at the net changes in job growth across all countries, the categories with the highest percentage job growth net of automation include the following:

- healthcare providers
- professionals such as engineers, scientists, accountants, and analysts
- IT professionals and other technology specialists
- managers and executives, whose work cannot easily be replaced by machines
- educators, especially in emerging economies with young populations
- "creatives," a small but growing category of artists, performers, and entertainers who will be in demand as rising incomes create more demand for leisure and recreation
- builders and related professions, particularly in the scenario that involves higher investments in infrastructure and buildings

manual and service jobs in unpredictable environments, such as home-health aides and gardeners. (https://www.mckinsey.com/global-themes/future-of-organizations-and-work/what-the-future-of-work-will-mean-for-jobs-skills-and-wages)

Pittsburgh is an interesting case of what an urban area needs to go through in contemporary times. The city was a prime example of a loser to industrialized robotics and world competition. The city, historically known for steel production, soon became a significant part of the Rust Belt, while Japan and China became serious strong competitors in the steel industry. By an odd circumstance, people in Pittsburgh became primary innovators and creators of robotics. Pittsburgh today is, ironically speaking, a modern center of robotic invention and engineering. Katz and Nowak summarize the Pittsburgh experience:

> Economic growth is a precondition for urban prosperity, but old models of growth are insufficient in today's global economy. Pittsburgh's renaissance—from a rust belt victim of deindustrialization to a high-tech global hub—is a prime example of what is needed, a model that differentiates a regional economy globally and prioritizes long-term investments in innovation assets, talent, and quality places. (Katz and Nowak 2017, 59)

The Katz and Nowak study indicated Pittsburgh's development in the robotics industry began with the 1979 nuclear power plant catastrophe at Three-Mile Island, near Pittsburgh. A scholar and a team of graduate students at Carnegie Mellon University invented and designed robots to explore the nuclear reactors' basement and assess the character and extent of damage so that no human beings needed to enter that area. The irony lies in the fact that, as a city that once declined, today, with the help of Carnegie Mellon University, the University of Pittsburgh, and the Westinghouse and Bechtel corporations, it is now profiting from the rise of robotic manufacturing.

A recent study of the Brookings Institute describes robotics in manufacturing centers throughout the United States. They offer a nationwide map of robotic location, shown in figure 5.1.

Today, robotic arms have been devised to help the military dismantle explosive devices in war zones, and local bomb squads can do the same domestically. Robots have been developed in medicine to "help people with disabilities better navigate the logistics of a world not designed to accommodate them."[31] Trashbot is on the market, a robot that separates recyclables from waste.

Figure 5.1. Where the robots are

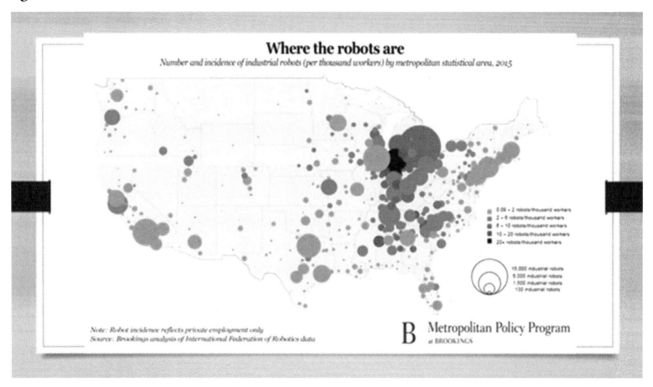

A more recent study by Leigh and Kraft in *Regional Studies* provides the geographic distribution robotic establishments and employment by metropolitan areas. This is shown in table 5.1. This study reaffirms the geographic pattern of robotics shown in the map above. There is a heavy concentration in the Midwest. However, there also significant coastal urban areas: Seattle, Boston, Los Angeles, and New York.

---

[31] *Pittsburgh Post-Gazette*, January 2, 2015.

Table 5.1. Robotic manufacturing in establishments and employment by urban region in the United States

Source: https://www.citylab.com/life/2018/07/americas-new-robot-geography/564155/?utm_source=nl__link2_071218&silverid=MzMzMTY0NDQ5MjUzS0&utm_source=citylab-daily&silverid=MzMzMTY0NDQ5MjUzS0.
Derived from: Leigh, M. G., and B. R. Kraft. 2018. "Emerging Robotic Regions in the United States: Insights for regional economic evolution." *Regional Studies* 52, no. 6: 804–14.

Urban Region	Total Employment	Integrator Employment	Manufacturer Employment
Milwaukee-Wakesha-West Allis, WI	8,971	8,874	97
Cleveland-Elyria, OH	8,411	8,198	213
Seattle-Tacoma-Bellevue, WA	5,367	5,302	65
Columbus, OH	5,351	358	4,993
Detroit-Warren-Dearborn, MI	3,012	1,762	1,250
Grand Rapids-Wyoming, MI	2,512	389	2,123
Chicago-Naperville-Elgin, IL-IN-WI2367	2,367	1,333	1,034
Minneapolis-St. Paul-Bloomington, MN-WI	2,265	849	1,416
Boston-Cambridge-Newton, MA-NH	2,068	287	1,781
Los Angeles-Long Beach-Anaheim, CA	1,513	564	949
Cincinnati, OH-KY-IN	1,391	704	687
New York-Newark-Jersey City, NY-NJ-PA	1,192	121	1,071
Kansas City, MO-KS	835	835	0

Urban Region	Total Employment	Integrator Employment	Manufacturer Employment
Iowa City, IA	750	750	0
Pittsburgh, PA	715	190	525
San Jose-Sunnyvale-Santa Clara, CA	656	76	580
Akron, OH	634	600	34
Philadelphia-Camden-Wilmington, PA-NJ-DE-MD	610	254	356
Wapakoneta, OH	600	600	0
Charlotte-Concord-Gastonia, NC-SC	556	287	269
Houston-The Woodlands-Sugarland, TX	552	407	145
Atlanta	460	240	220
Dallas	380	152	228
Birmingham	331	81	250

Energy

Traditional energy has been dominant for more than a century. Petroleum and coal still provide the predominant natural resources for heating, cooling, electricity, and transportation. At the time of this writing, despite efforts at creating energy sources that do not strongly emit greenhouse gas emissions, petroleum and coal are still dominant. In the 1970s, petroleum was largely brought from the Middle East. Today it is far more international. The largest petroleum companies in the world are found in China. The United States and Canada have found oil resources within their boundaries and within the Gulf of Mexico. It is one of Russia's major economic outputs.

The cost of petroleum reached a new high in the summer of 2008. Since that time, the costs have gone down considerably because of the more widespread geographic availability. This lowering of cost has meant an increasing destructive effect on global warming.

For the coal industry, however, trends have not been positive. While coal is still predominant in many countries, in the United States and other developed countries, their market share has been declining. This is a positive trend, as coal was certainly the leading source of greenhouse gas emissions and local pollution. As of this writing, the United States federal government has tried to create policies that will bring coal back to its previous contribution in energy supply. Market-wise, however, this does not appear to be happening.

Oil, of course, continues to be the dominant source of energy. It continues to dominate in heating, air-conditioning, and all forms of transportation. It continues to dominate in electricity production and industrial manufacturing. This domination continues to be worldwide. It also continues to be the predominant cause of global warming and local air pollution. It also appears to be a dominant oligopoly in all the OECD countries[32] as well as in China and Saudi Arabia. As noted in chapter 3, the leaking of oil is becoming more widespread and more damaging. Oil not only has market power but also has strong power in the political world.

Another source of energy is natural gas. Natural gas was first introduced in 1949, but the expanded production of today started in the early twenty-first century.

> Natural gas is a naturally occurring hydrocarbon gas mixture consisting primarily of methane, but commonly including varying amounts of other higher alkanes, and sometimes a small percentage of carbon dioxide, nitrogen, hydrogen sulfide, or helium. (Wikipedia)

---

[32] OECD is a forum of thirty-four industrialized countries that develops and promotes economic and social policies. The thirty-four OECD member countries are Australia, Austria, Belgium, Canada, Chile, Czech Republic, Denmark, Estonia, Finland, France, Germany, Greece, Hungary, Iceland, Ireland, Israel, Italy, Japan, Korea, Luxembourg, Mexico, the Netherlands, New Zealand, Norway, Poland, Portugal, Slovak Republic, Slovenia, Spain, Sweden, Switzerland, Turkey, the United Kingdom, and the United States.

Contemporary natural gas is released from subsurface porous rock formations through a process called hydraulic fracturing—or fracking. The production of natural gas from hydraulically fractured wells has come about through the technology of directional and horizontal drilling, which improved access to natural gas in tight rock formations.

Natural gas is used for electricity generation, heating, and cooling. It is also used in chemical manufacturing. It is used to a limited degree in automotive fuels. Natural gas is actually a more potent greenhouse gas than carbon dioxide due to the greater global warming potential of methane. The fracking process also has detrimental impacts on the local environment where it is extracted. The process uses large quantities of water that are then discharged with serious water pollution character. Today, natural gas is widely used globally. Russia exports natural gas to many countries in Europe and former Soviet territory.

There have been efforts at developing new technologies that can reduce reliance on coal, oil, and natural gas. Most prominent of these has been the development of solar panels that have recently become competitive market-wise. In the United States, this is encouraged by subsidy assistance, so many homeowners have installed panels on their roofs. Another technology designed to reduce dependence on oil is wind technology. In the United States, this has primarily been developed in the Midwest where there is extensive flat, prairie-type topography. Development of wind energy in oceanic areas has taken place in Europe (but only to a limited extent in the United States). Historically, there has long been the use of hydroelectric energy. This, of course, can pose environmental problems since it depends upon building dams on rivers, thereby creating damaging environmental effects in local areas.

Clearly, energy is a major global environmental problem involving the harnessing of energy, its distribution and its use. This is generally understood. People depend on their cars and need electricity and heat or air-conditioning in their homes. The substitute technologies need to make faster progress, especially in transportation. There are companies in both the US and China aiming to create self-driving and electric vehicles. While this is showing progress, it is not clear how quickly this work can have a meaningful impact on today's traffic congestion and widespread trucking and air travel.

Retail Activity

The last ten years have seen a significant shift in the way that people do shopping for equipment, gifts, clothing, and more. The rise of the Amazon Corporation has given new strength to mail order purchasing and delivery. This is showing some impact on major retailing operations. Amazon has established warehousing operations all over the United States. Consequently, one can buy clothing, jewelry, cell phones, books, and more and have them delivered within one to two days. This has significantly altered the way people do shopping.

Historically, early 20th Century shopping meant going to an urban, downtown, central business area and visiting the stores there. After World War II, mall shopping was created in suburban areas, and it later expanded with big-box stores such as Walmart, Costco, and Target. In the late nineteenth and early twentieth centuries, mail order shopping was oriented to helping people in rural areas and was identified by the mail order catalogs of Sears Roebuck, Montgomery Ward, and others. Prices might have been lower than in a downtown store or suburban mall, but delivery time often meant a long wait. Today, with FedEx and UPS in addition to the United States Postal Service, Amazon, with a national multitude of warehouses, can deliver an order within one or two days. They deliver their Kindle e-books in a matter of seconds.

This change in activity has both positive and negative effects. To the extent that mail order shopping can reduce the use of automobiles and lower traffic congestion, it offers a positive environmental effect. It is not clear, however, what effects such a shopping system has on trucking. Quick delivery does rely on many large, well-stocked warehousing operations and increased trucking.

One can see a possible important impact on the urbanization process. Amazon's business is likely to impact central city shopping areas as well as suburban malls and the big-box development. Several recent major store closings have indicated that the effect of Amazon's business is clearly being felt. Macy's, JC Penney, Sears, and other major stores have had several store closings, although they may still have strong retail business activity.[33]

---

[33] Sears announced it was going out of business in January 2019.

Technology and Agriculture

A key area for meeting the challenges of a significantly increased urban population, along with an economic system that gives little attention to global warming or environmental dangers, is the agricultural patterns for providing food for expanding urban populations. Beyond this problem, farming has also become clearly identified as an environmental problem. There are three aspects to the problem.

First, the major aquifers in the world are being seriously depleted of water. The National Geographic magazine in 2016 had a comprehensive article on how the largest aquifer in the United States (the Ogallala) has been undergoing water depletion. Corn farming, livestock, and other forms of farming are causing the depletion. It is an aquifer that runs from South Dakota south to Texas. Only in Nebraska is a water supply still adequate.

As the author, Laura Parker noted in her article in the National Geographic:

> "All the Earth's continents contain aquifers, several larger than the Ogallala. By the beginning of the 21st century, a third of the world depended on aquifers for drinking water and farming. In China, plagued by drought, the North China Plain aquifer sustains 117 million people in Beijing and surrounding areas. Similar aquifers in the Ganges Brahmaputra Basin and the Indus Basin have helped lead to a population boom that will cause India to pass China as the world's most populous nation by 2022." (Parker, 2016)

Aquifers in several of the world's most heavily populated regions are being depleted at precipitous rates. NASA satellites, monitoring changes in Earth's gravitational pull, found that 21 of the world's 37 largest aquifers have passed the sustainable tipping point. Clearly adequate provision of food for population that will be two thirds urban in 2050 is already in danger.

The second aspect of today's agricultural problems lies in the runoff from agricultural activities along with livestock waste creating serious contamination of streams, rivers and lakes. I live in the American state with 10,000 lakes and the issue of water pollution from farming has been under strong debate in the last

7-8 years. An effort to require a buffer zone of only 50 feet from adjoining water bodies has become a major source of strong political disagreement. Economics for farmers almost everywhere is extremely difficult, and those in Minnesota clearly argue these buffers will seriously hurt them financially.[34]

The third factor is serious deforestation occurring globally. Some deforestation occurs because of increasing tropical storms particularly those recently in the Caribbean where serious forest loss occurred in Dominica and Puerto Rico. As stated by Brad Plumer in a recent New York Times article:

> "In all, the world's tropical forests lost roughly 39 million acres of trees last year, an
> area roughly the size of Bangladesh, according to a report Wednesday by Global Forest
> Watch that used new satellite data from the University of Maryland." (Brad Plumer,
> New York Times, June 27, 2018, page A6)

A significant cause of deforestation was seen in Brazil with farmers and ranchers clearing land for agriculture by setting forest fires.[35] This was also true in Columbia so that the Amazon Forest region spiked in clearing in 2017.

Clearly, the combination of all factors influencing agriculture suggests strong need for technological innovation if we are to provide food adequately over the next 20 to 30 years. The growing urban population, the increasing depletion of water aquifer resources, and the increasing contamination of surface water resources by farming clearly pose very significant sustainable development problems. Given the forecasts of urban population, is it possible to provide the necessary food for that population? Rural decline also signifies a decline in labor force for agricultural activity. Agricultural technology clearly is a high priority in the pursuit of sustainable development. Can there really be the food to feed a predominantly urban world?

There is growing scientific and engineering research concerning food supply in the future. A recent web page, from the organization Business Insider, provides an inventory of current research going on in the agriculture field. (http://www.businessinsider.com/15-emerging-agriculture-technologies-2014-4) Their

---

[34] Also hurting famers at the time of this writing is the tariff war between U.S. and China

[35] Brazil recently elected a President who has indicated that he will allow intrusion into the Amazon rain forest.

listing signifies the technological advances that are financially viable in agricultural markets today and the next few years. Their work suggests that we can visualize food production that routinely uses highly sophisticated technologies such as robots, temperature and moisture sensors, aerial images, and GPS technology. Also available are air and soil sensors, equipment maintenance, global positioning systems and GIS mapping software. Building on geolocation technologies, future control could save on seed, minerals, fertilizer and herbicides by reducing overlapping inputs.

Future opportunities include extensive use of robots that can substitute for human laborers in the processes of harvesting, fruit picking, ploughing, soil maintenance, weeding, planting, irrigation, etc. Also seen in the near future is the use of satellite imagery and advanced sensors. For urban planners, one of the more interesting ideas is the idea of vertical urban farming. This would provide opportunity to do farming in urban skyscrapers. For some time, this has been considered beneficial to provide floral and vegetable gardening on the top of urban structures. However, the ideas suggested in the Business Insider web page would seem to suggest food gardening at various levels of skyscraper balconies.

The use of new technology in the agricultural business is reported to be high. It tends to be dominant in use by younger professional farmers, but older farmers are also increasing their use of new technology (http://www.krishijagran.com/news/is-it-that-new-generation-of-farmers-only-use-new-technology/). Clearly, artificial intelligence and robotics would seem potentially helpful for food provision given the perspective rise of urban population. What is still open to discussion, however, is the dominant role of the oligopoly firms such as Monsanto-Bayer and DowDuPont as well as the growing oligopolies in food marketing.

Warfare Technology

One of the most disturbing aspects of the contemporary world of innovation and creativity is that of the military. It is true that many useful inventions emerged from World War II and became a part of our civilian life. These include radar, microwave ovens, recording tape, and other innovations converted from military to civilian use.

Understandably, a strong military would be very happy if a war could be fought without sending in human troops. The United States seems to be moving in this direction. The US has military forces as of this writing in many different nations, including Africa and the Middle East and especially Afghanistan and Syria. Drone aircraft are increasingly used as bomber instruments. Thus, the destruction of enemy personnel, equipment, and whole cities can take place without risk to American bomber pilots or their staffs.

However, the potentiality of enemies stealing or otherwise acquiring the latest warfare equipment means this pursuit of robotic weapons is not wholly optimistic. Nor will these new weapons necessarily be limited to the activities of a declared war. In the US, war armaments are available and sold commercially to the general public, such as the AR-15 rifle. For a time, local municipal police departments in the United States acquired surplus military equipment.

Historically, wars were fought in the open fields of rural areas. Even World War I was so located. Today, war is carried out in urban areas, reflecting the real advantages of robotic equipment. Advancing the technology of war equipment is not likely to eliminate future wars. War is destructive not only to human lives but also to natural environment resources.

In addition, the past few years have seen a new form of warfare—cybernetic warfare. The most publicized of this warfare involved investigating the Russian effort to interfere in the United States presidential election of 2016. This has also been a focus of attention in Russian interference in European affairs. This is an effort by one country to influence who might become a leader in another country, thereby seeking to influence international relations. Cybernetic warfare is also being used in global economic affairs.

Recently another incident of Cyberwar effort came by way of Facebook, where a London artificial intelligence firm, Cambridge Analytica, developed detailed personal information about eighty-seven million Americans in the hopes of influencing their political voting. Many more instances of Cyberwar battling have taken place. The credit firm Equifax was also invaded by persons using artificial intelligence to steal credit information. In effect, today's communication technology has opened not only to broad social communication but also to digitized, electronic means of stealing or invading privacy. What really distinguishes cybernetic warfare is that it substitutes machines for workers, capital for labor, and brains for brawn.

Technological Innovation and Its Impact on the Labor Force

Probably the most important feature of today's technology lies in how it has changed the way people are employed. A recent study by the Brookings Institute illustrates this dramatically. Their Metropolitan Policy Program study shows how different long-standing occupations have changed and require increasing education in the digitalization process to be able to work today. Their first discussion of this is pictured in figure 5.2. From this image, it is obvious that computer scientists, software developers, and computer systems analysts require a high level of digitalization skill, and this has been the case for many years. However, to be a financial analyst (a banker, an asset manager, a stockbroker, a hedge fund analyst) today requires a high level of digitalization skill. Digital equipment is now a fundamental tool.

What the Brookings Institute authors describe as medium-range digitalization, I consider somewhat simplified. Not only do registered nurses need digitalization skills, but everyone in the medical profession depends highly on this. In addition, of course, every form of repairing communications or heating or plumbing equipment requires some level of digitalization education.[36]

The detailed Brookings study actually looked at 455 occupations, so that generalizations pictured here can essentially provide a relatively accurate overall picture of the impact of technology on the labor force.

Early characterizations of an economy signified three areas: agriculture, industry, and service. What was inadequate was the characterization "service." Years ago, service workers included everybody from a restaurant waiter to a lawyer or accountant. Sassen, in her recent book, has helped more clearly differentiate

---

[36] I also have some concern about other occupations involving a low relationship to digitalization skills. Security guards today are very likely to rely on one or another form of artificial intelligence to improve the guarding of buildings, factories, and so on. I suspect even chefs and cooks might have some relationship to artificial intelligence resources

service occupations. People who work in the highly digitized occupations are indeed service workers, but their extensive education and skills in law, accounting, and venture capital are used most in the work they do. In effect, they have strong influences on all economic, social, and political behavior. The third and declining group in the Brookings Institute study needs only low levels of digitalized education.

Figure 5.2. Digitalization requirements by occupation

Mark Muro et al. 2017. *Digitalization and the American Workforce.* Brookings Institute. https://www.brookings.edu/research/digitalization-and-the-american-workforce/.

The Brookings study highlights the fact that employment is changing over time and that the occupations with high digitized skill are seeing rapidly growing employment, while those in the low digitized occupations are seeing rapidly diminished job opportunities. Figure 5.2 illustrates changes in employment levels between 2002 and 2016.[37]

The Brookings study shows that between 2002 and 2016, the shares of US jobs and employment requiring digital knowledge rose significantly. Artificial intelligence and robotic developments not only have enhanced communication and transactional skills but also have had positive effects on economic productivity. The negative effects, however, create significant present and future economic, social, and educational problems.

The changes over a short period have been dramatic. Since 2002, the share of all US jobs that require extensive digital skills surged from 5 percent to 23 percent in 2016. Midlevel digital skills surged from 40 to 48 percent of the total. Meanwhile, since 2010, nearly four million of the nation's thirteen million new jobs created—30 percent of them—have required high-level digital skills. The decline of jobs not requiring digital skills dipped from 56 percent in 2005 to less than a third (30 percent) in 2016.

[37] Brookings Institute Metropolitan Program study builds on a detailed analysis of changes in the digital content of 545 occupations covering 90 percent of the US workforce in all industries since 2001. Looking broadly across the job roles, digitalization scores rose in 517 of 545 analyzed occupations from 2002 to 2016. The average digitalization score across all occupations rose from 29 in 2002 to 46 in 2016, a 57 percent increase.

Figure 5.3. Employment by levels of job digitalization

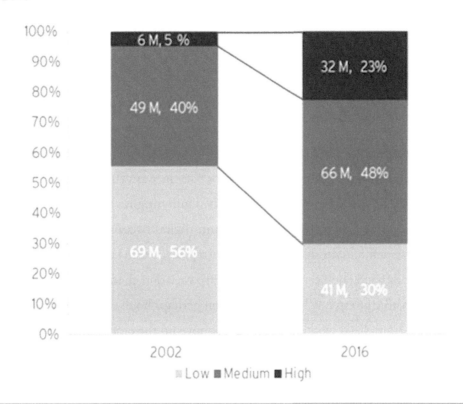

Employment by levels of job digitalization
2002 and 2016

	2002	2016
High	6 M, 5 %	32 M, 23%
Medium	49 M, 40%	66 M, 48%
Low	69 M, 56%	41 M, 30%

■ Low ■ Medium ■ High

Source: Brookings analysis of O*NET and OES data

Mark Muro et al. 2017. *Digitalization and the American Workforce.* Brookings Institute. https://www.brookings.edu/research/digitalization-and-the-american-workforce/.

Digitalization is associated with increased pay and job resiliency. Across the skills continuum, employees are rewarded for the depth and breadth of their digital skills through increased wages. Workers in occupations with medium or high digital skills in 2016 were paid significantly more than those in low-digital occupations. The digitalization of the US economy appears to be contributing to the hollowing out and divergence of historic employment and wage distributions.

The extent of digitalization also varies widely across urban areas and is strongly linked with variations in regional economic performance. In geographical terms, digitalization is happening everywhere, but its progress varies widely across the map. In almost all cases, metropolitan areas saw their mean digitalization score increase by twelve to eighteen points, meaning that, for the most part, digital laggards among metros were catching up to the digital leaders, allowing for metro digital scores to converge somewhat.

Digitalization is creating new race- and gender-based training challenges. The mean skills ratings of the jobs occupied by workers in major demographic groups vary in ways that almost certainly contribute to those groups' uneven access to opportunity. Women, with slightly higher aggregate scores as a group than men, dominate employment in many of the largest medium-digital occupational groups, such as in health professions. By contrast, women remain significantly underrepresented in such digital positions as computer and mathematical occupations and engineering. Equally sharp variation characterizes the employment profiles of the nation's racial and ethnic groups. While digitalization perhaps holds out possible opportunities for less educated or historically marginalized workers or groups to move up the employment ladder, too few of them yet appear to be attaining that progress. Asian workers are high in holding digitizing jobs, African workers are high in the medical professions, and African American and Latin workers are still predominantly in low-digitized occupations.

Innovative, creative work in artificial intelligence and robotics is having significant economic, social, political, and educational impacts on the world today. Right up with the United States are China and India. Similarly, the European Union (particularly Germany) is also heavily engaged in innovative development. The final designed physical instruments are manufactured worldwide and produced in low-labor-cost countries. Using the instruments has helped create sophisticated networks that enhance corporate power and control. This also promotes advanced education. At the same time, digitalization has shifted ordinary employment opportunities that enlarge and promote inequality. Digitized capacities have enlarged scientific understanding and increased understanding of climate and environmental difficulties but has yet to promote adequate action incentives to address these problems.

Figure 5.4. Mean digital score by metropolitan area, 2016

https://www.brookings.edu/research/digitalization-and-the-american-workforce/

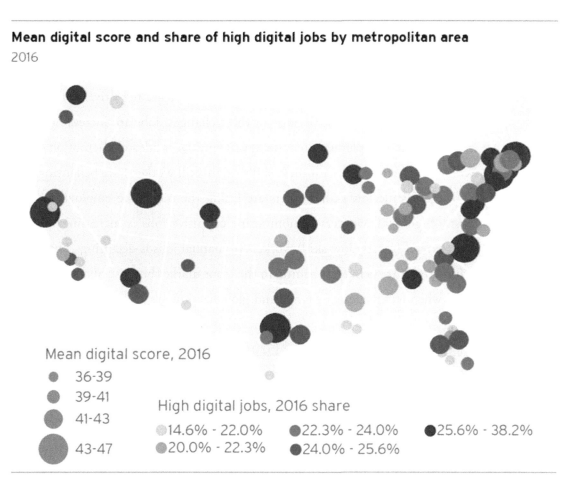

Mean digital score and share of high digital jobs by metropolitan area

2016

Mean digital score, 2016

- 36-39
- 39-41
- 41-43
- 43-47

High digital jobs, 2016 share

- 14.6% - 22.0%
- 20.0% - 22.3%
- 22.3% - 24.0%
- 24.0% - 25.6%
- 25.6% - 38.2%

Source: Brookings analysis of O*Net and OES data

A more recent publication of the World Bank indicates technology innovation is also having an impact on labor in the European Union. The report says that technological change is having an impact in providing ever more opportunities for well-skilled workers while leaving low-skilled workers behind. Automation, 3-D printing, and artificial intelligence are changing the nature of Europe's jobs, with a growing importance of nonroutine, cognitive, and analytical work. The following was stated in the World Bank report:

> Jobs across the EU are increasingly about cognitive and interpersonal tasks, while manual and routine tasks are declining. These trends have, for now, been less marked in Central and Eastern European countries, where routine cognitive tasks are still growing slightly, reflecting a less advanced stage of structural change. Technological change, offshoring and the skills upgrading of the workforce are big drivers of the changes in the task content of jobs. Because of these changes, jobs are increasingly intensive in skills that complement technology (cognitive and social-emotional skills …). Workers well equipped with these skills (high-skill workers) are benefiting from these changes, while low-skill workers are losing the most: the employment share of (mostly high-skill) workers in nonroutine cognitive jobs is increasing the most, and the share of (mostly low-skill) workers in manual jobs is declining. Thus, low-income Europeans are being left behind in the labor market because of their low skills, at a time when technological change and globalization are making jobs more skill intensive.
> (http://pubdocs.worldbank.org/en/244481520499464074/Growing-United-v03-online-18-03-08.pdf, page 23)

Conclusion

Unambiguously, new technology is at the heart of human activity today. It aids in economic growth, it is fundamental to urban growth, and it is a challenge for educating coming generations. There are potentials for having new technological environments that would successfully meet the challenges I have described in earlier chapters. However, our ability to predict the future is not really enhanced. The recent killing of a pedestrian by a self-driving automobile poses questions about the future of robotic automobiles and buses. The serious depletion of water resources for agriculture and food production are not seriously addressed in new agricultural technology. The rising cyber warfare and its attacks on individual information and integrity cannot be considered positive unless there is serious counter innovation and creativity. Clearly, current political relationships in the world make everyone insecure in terms of the possibilities of future war, with key countries upgrading their nuclear and other weapons.

Putting war aside, however, there is great variability in how these new technologies will affect the United Nations' pursuit of the seventeen sustainable-development goals. We can be optimistic concerning many of them, but there are still issues that are not being focused on (and, in reality, may be worsened). The 2050 level of urban population, for example, is not being tackled through technological activity. Basic human difficulties in urban environments—poverty; discrimination and hate on the grounds of sex, race, and religion; and severe inequality—are not being improved by today's artificial intelligence and robotics (Gough 2017).

There is evidence that a major part of the progress of technological change has been aided and abetted by the corporatist, oligopolistic economy. Corporate entities that barely existed in the year 2000 are now dominating the world of artificial intelligence—Google, Facebook, Microsoft, Apple, Samsung, Amazon. The combined psychological motivations of greed and power are still strongly linked. As Herman Daly has argued (1996 and 2014), along with Jeffrey Sachs (2015), an oligopolistic-corporatist economy only leads us toward a future of more destructive climate change and environmental ruin.

References

Castells, M. 2010. *The Rise of the Network Society.* 2nd ed. Chichester, UK: Wiley-Blackwell.

Daly, Herman. 2014. *From Uneconomic Growth to a Steady-State Economy.* Cheltenham, UK: Edward Elgar.

Daly, Herman. 1996. *Beyond Growth: The Economics of Sustainable Development.* Boston: Beacon Press.

Gough, I. 2017. *Heat, Greed and Human Need: Climate Change, Capitalism and Sustainable Well Being.* Cheltenham, UK: Edward Elgar Publishing.

Grassi, M. J., and P. Schrimpf. 2017. "Top 10 Most Intriguing Technologies in Agriculture." http://www.precisionag.com/systems-management/top-10-most-intriguing-technologies-in-agriculture/.

Katz, B., and J. Nowak. 2017. *The New Localism: How Cities Can Thrive in the Age of Populism.* Washington, DC: Brookings Institute Press.

Muro, M., S. Liu, J. Whiiton, and S. Kukarni. 2017. *Digitalization and the American Workforce.* Washington, DC: Brookings Institute.

Plumer, B. 2018. "Near-Record Tree Loss Seen in Tropical Forests Last Year." *New York Times*, June 27, page A6.

Ridao-Cano, C., and C. Bodewig. 2018. *Growing United: Upgrading Europe's Convergence Machine.* Washington, DC: World Bank Report on the European Union.

Roos, K. 2018. "His 2020 Slogan: Beware of Robots." *New York Times*, February 11, 2018.

Sachs, J. D. 2015. *The Age of Sustainable Development.* New York: Columbia University Press.

Sassen, S. 2012. *Cities in a World Economy.* 4th ed. Los Angeles: Pine Forge Press (Sage).

Chapter 6

The Atmosphere of Future Urban Development

Given the trends described in previous chapters, what will the urban life of planet Earth be like in 2030, 2050, or 2100? As populations vacate the rural areas and move to urban areas, as corporate giants tend to dominate not only the economic world but also governance institutions, and as new technologies of artificial technology and robotics permeate all living conditions, what will be the nature, character, and livability of the planet's urbanity?

Chapter 2 reported the significant population forecasts prepared by the United Nations in 2014. A reminder: by 2030, close to 60 percent (or close to an added billion) of the world population will be urban, and by 2050, 66 percent will be urban (an additional 2.5 billion from today). In OECD countries, population growth between now and 2050 is forecast to be 130 million people, suggesting the insightful need for thirty-five to forty million more new housing units. In the less developed countries, there will be 2.3 billion more people, suggesting the need for construction of six hundred to seven hundred million more housing units.

Chapter 3 offered no direct or substantive forecasts of the world economy. The combination of greed and power characterize the economy today, and one could easily surmise that combination may easily continue, along with inequality. As the economy is strongly linked to urbanization, economic greed and power will likely have strong influences on the nature of future urban communities. Chapter 4 suggests a future need for more convincing, inclusive government leadership, and chapter 5 offers images of future technologies creating a living atmosphere of highly different character (including significantly decreased demand for human labor). Clearly, there needs to be insightful forms of institutional revision and interventions oriented toward sustainable ecological urban economy.

The process of urban population growth obviously implies significant increases in urban land and land use, urban housing neighborhoods, urban transportation, and urban infrastructure. There will be increasing need for potable water and effective waste management, along with increasing demand for food. Urban growth also demands new or expanded electric generators and grid systems, communications networks, factories, schools, hospitals, and shopping facilities. Consequently, this chapter explores the potentialities of planning for this growth in an atmosphere of corporatist, oligopolistic economics, weakened democracies, and increasing growth of authoritative countries. At the root of this question is the issue of significant financial requirements to meet the housing and infrastructure needs of future generations. Where will these financial resources be found and who will be the decision makers controlling them?

The problem is described in a quote from Bret Boyd, a corporate business executive with experience in the energy, technology, and finance sectors:

> The impact of urbanization falls into three primary categories. The first is _infrastructure_, as public officials and city planners need to build infrastructure to support larger populations in a sustainable fashion, _which private companies will ultimately build and manage._ Second are _private development companies_, which compete with their peers to build and manage large dwellings, venues, and facilities that people live, shop, eat, and are entertained in. The third are _consumer products companies_ that sell goods and services to people whose consumption patterns are influenced by where and how they live. (Emphasis added.)

Boyd goes on to say:

> Another driver is the shape of modern economies, specifically the *increasing concentration of wealth creation* and the specialized nature of modern workforces. When wealth is concentrated in smaller groups and more occupations revolve around products and services that support these centers of wealth creation, there is a natural pull towards those centers.
> (https://graylinegroup.com/urbanization-catalyst-overview/) (Emphasis added.)

In short, the world is projected to build more and more urban settings, but how will this happen given the increasing trends of inequality fostered by today's corporatist economics and its supremacy over government influence? Past urban development since the industrial age has meant significant, ongoing environmental damage, so that today we need combined global and local remedies to stop the Tragedy of the Commons.

Historically, corporations in the United States, Europe, and other developed nations have had varying but dominant roles in the land-development process. In the United States, the government regulatory role after World War II was highly localized. Local governments, with state-government sanction, increased their interest in planning and regulating development within their local jurisdiction. Local ordinances focused on zoning and subdivision control. At that time, realtors and homebuilders also tended to be local businesses. In the 1950s, I served on a local planning board in a suburb of Boston. Postwar urban sprawl was very much underway, yet virtually every builder applying to build homes was headquartered within thirty miles of our town hall. Moreover, their sources of capital also tended to be local banks or financing firms.

In Europe at that time, the task was rebuilding urban areas that had been devastated in the war. There was help from the United States through the Marshall Plan. This was described by the Brookings Institute, which was actively involved in designing the program:

> In the wake of World War II, the United States did something almost unprecedented in world history: It launched and paid for an economic aid plan to restore a continent reeling from war. The European Recovery Plan—better known as the Marshall Plan,

after chief advocate Secretary of State George C. Marshall—was in part an act of charity but primarily an act of self-interest, intended to prevent postwar Western Europe from succumbing to communism. By speeding the recovery of Europe and establishing the basis for NATO and diplomatic alliances that endure to this day, it became one of the most successful U.S. government programs ever. (https://www.brookings.edu/book/the-marshall-plan-and-the-shaping-of-american-strategy/)

Great Britain, for example, created a Garden Cities New Towns program (Rodwin 1956) as well as the reconstruction of London. In Holland, the central government was instrumental in the rebuilding of Rotterdam. Global corporatism was not dominant at that time. Local business organizations were usually involved in public-private cooperative arrangements, with strong involvement from professional architects and planners. Not only were local construction firms involved, but so were private citizens. The program helped important damaged cities from World War II, including Dresden, Berlin, Rotterdam, London, Bremen, Würzburg, and Hamburg.

Today, such government support of rebuilding urbanity has pretty much faded.[38] Urban development is predominantly a business operation, and the only exception is that of a local government, in various ways, trying to provide affordable housing, education, and medical help for the poor and reduction of police crime activity. Corporate real estate plays the dominant role in urban development, maintenance, and growth. Government provides infrastructure along with social enhancement programs (health, education). Corporate real estate relies heavily on finance oligopolies in providing urban land for manufacturing and service oligopolies. The Bret Boyd description quoted above is a candid portrayal of the urban building process of today and tomorrow—unless there are means for inserting new forces.

Ashley Dawson (2017) in his recent book provides clear illustration of the dominant role of the wealthy in determining the character of an urban community. His argument is that this dominant role overcomes potential means of protection from rising oceanic levels and torrential rainstorms and hurricanes. In his

---

[38] Of course, the warfare destruction of urbanity has not vanished. Middle East cities still provide visions of large-scale urban destruction.

first chapter, he describes patterns of development in Miami, Florida, and New York City, where hurricanes clearly demonstrated areas of potential future damage. Yet in both cities, what one saw was development of luxury high-rise apartment towers, providing the wealthy a site with marvelous residential views of the cities' harbors. Dawson suggests the following:

> All too often, such plans promote processes of 'environmental gentrification,' where green living is used to attract wealthy professionals to luxury buildings in freshly developed urban neighborhoods, rather than fostering urban sustainability and environmental justice for the majority of citizens. (Dawson 2018, Kindle location 663)

Additionally, the corporate world will continue to dominate in determining the urban locations of corporate activity. This, of course, can be seen the world over. Location and design of central business districts and of suburban business districts will continue to be dominated by corporate interests. This often also dictates the construction of infrastructure. I recall a visit to Cincinnati, where the federal interstate highway through the city had an exit ramp built directly – and only – into a single corporate office building.

Housing

City Of Mozambique. Guillem Sartario/Agence France Presse—Getty Images

In a recent speech, Cédric Van Styvendael, president of the organization Housing Europe, raised the substantive question of today's global world: "Housing as a Human Right Vs. Housing as a Commodity—Redefining the Roles of Public & Private Sectors."[39] Globally today, housing is very much not a human right but a commodity.

The greatest problem facing growing urbanization throughout the world is that of housing. Even in the United States, there is an expectation of forty million more residents in 2030. Assuming two to four persons per household, this would mean the construction of some ten to twenty million residences among the 536 US metropolitan areas by 2030.

One reason why housing is a top priority is the question of how global dwellings will be provided. This is debatable in terms of the interaction between private business and governments (national, regional, and local).

Housing is difficult, particularly the process of who decides what to build, when and where, and at what cost. Given the projected future demands, this will likely become an increasingly complex issue. Is it the role of the private market, or is it the role of the government? Or does it require collaboration of both business and government? At what level are decisions made—national, regional, or local? In the United States, decisions are primarily made by the private market having private land ownership, with a limited local oversight, primarily utilizing local zoning law. In other parts of world, the private business organizations face stronger governmental influence. However, in some truly impoverished places, there is neither government nor private market control. People in search of housing can only use their own physical abilities to access scrap materials to give them self-built shelter. Needed infrastructure is absent, including roads, water supply, and sanitation.

These institutional relationships vary from country to country. I will start off with the United States and then examine potential future housing policies in Europe, China, India, and Africa.

Housing in the United States

In the United States, the real estate industry involves widespread cooperation between different business actors. Figure 6.1 provides a basic outline of the institutional framework for the provision of housing in the

---

[39] This is comparable to the political debate in health care: is health care a human right or a business?

United States. The diagram strongly suggests a pattern of behavior among a variety of business interests—behavior that tends to reinforce class and racial divisions in the housing market. For the most part, housing provision requirements tend to be carried out by local businesses, except for those on the right-hand side of the diagram. Insurance companies, title companies, credit companies, and investment banks play important roles, especially in growing urban regions. These financial institutions can be both local and international, small and very large. During the period of early urban sprawl after World War II, these organizations tended to be strictly small and local. Over the years, larger and larger corporations have become dominant in real estate finance, so that local developers will likely turn to national (or international) financiers.

There is evidence that real estate development in almost every United States city is moving toward corporate concentration and power. One example was briefly referred to in the discussion of the Berkshire Hathaway Corporation in chapter 3. In September 2017, two Berkshire Hathaway firms (*Long and Foster* and *Home Services Corporation*) were merged, creating a powerful business involving home sales, mortgages, titles, insurance, and escrow deals in thirty states, more than half the country.

Recent signals suggest strong corporate influence of land use. An early signal was provided by Mark Weiss (1987) in his book about the American real estate industry. A more recent publication by Peter Brown (2015) also covers the thinking developers follow in the urban development process. There is also an indication, however, that the development industry is moving toward creating some level of oligopoly.

Builder magazine provides an annual list of America's biggest builders (www.builderonline.com). The list includes the one hundred largest builders in the United States. Table 6.1 shows the top ten homebuilders in 2015, spreading across many states. The top-ranked Horton Company occupies seventy-eight markets in twenty-six states. Third-ranked Pultegroup operates in fifty markets in twenty-five states. There is also evidence that one of the ten focuses more on high-priced homes. The Toll Brothers ranked tenth in closings but ranked sixth in million-dollar revenues.

Overall, housing decisions in the United States are still made by private entrepreneurs subject to limited local control. While still predominantly local in nature, builders and buyers are increasingly relying on national and international financing corporations to instill the presence of capital. This was a major source leading to the Great Recession in 2008–2010. Banks combined individual subprime mortgage documents into venture capital instruments, at which point these failed and the United States faced a major mortgage foreclosure process, estimated at more than one million housing unit foreclosures.

Overall, despite the ups and downs of the US housing market in the twenty-first century, it seems evident the financial oligopoly (banking, investment, titles, etc.) will be very much involved in shaping the housing market in the United States in the coming years.

Notwithstanding this, housing has become a serious problem in the United States since the Great Recession. A recent report by the Pew Charitable Trust provides current information about rent-burdened households throughout the United States. "Rent-burdened" households refers to households paying more than 30 percent of their income for housing. "Severely rent-burdened" refers to those households paying more than 50 percent of their income.

The summary of the Pew Charitable Trust findings are as follows:

- In 2015, 38 percent of all "renter households" were rent burdencd, an increase of about 19 percent from 2001.
- The share of renter households that were severely rent burdened—spending 50 percent or more of monthly income on rent—increased by 42 percent between 2001 and 2015, to 17 percent.
- In 2015, 46 percent of African-American-led renter households were rent burdened, compared with 34 percent of white households. Between 2001 and 2015, the gap between the share of white and African- American households experiencing severe rent burden grew by 66 percent.
- Senior-headed renter households are more likely than those headed by people in other age groups to be rent burdened. In 2015, about 50 percent of renter families headed by someone 65 or older were rent burdened, and more than a fifth were severely rent burdened. (Pew Charitable Trust 2018, 4–5)

Table 6.1. Top ten homebuilders in the United States

Source: www.builderonline.com.

Rank	Company	2 0 1 5 Closings	2015 Gross Revenue (Millions)	Number of States in Business	Markets
1	D. R. Horton	36,736	$10,938	26	78
2	Lennar Corporation	24,292	$9,474	19	40
3	Pultegroup	17,127	$5,982	25	50
4	NVR	13,326	$5,159	15	42
5	Calatlantic Group	12,560	$5,280	17	41
6	KB Home	8,196	$3,032	8	25
7	Meritage Homes	6,522	$2,579	9	22
8	Taylor Morrison	6,311	$2,977	9	17
9	Hovnanian Enterprises	5,757	$2,264	14	45
10	Toll Brothers	5,525	$5,525	19	50

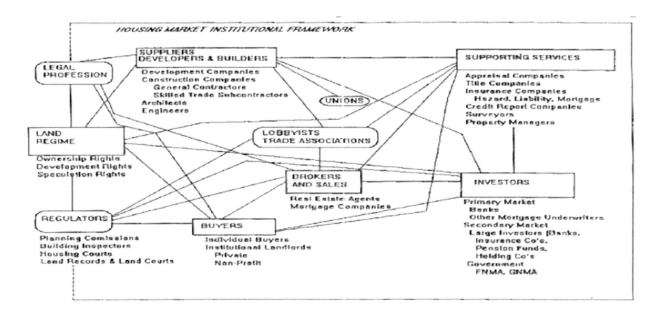

Figure 6.1. US housing market institutional framework

From: Bolan, R. S. 1999. "Social Interaction and Institutional Design: The Case of Housing in the United States." In *The Revival of Strategic Spatial Planning*. Edited by W. Salet and A. Faludi. Royal Netherlands Academy of Arts and Science. Figure 1, p. 30.

Housing in Europe

A recent report, *The State of Housing in Europe 2017*, provides the following summary of the decline in the European housing market (http://www.housingeurope.eu/resource-1000/the-state-of-housing-in-the-eu-2017):

- Residential construction as a share of GDP is currently [2017] just over half than its 2006 level, and construction is recovering much slower than prices. …
- High building standards and requirements are posing a significant challenge to the provision of social and affordable housing in several countries, …
- Because of construction not keeping up with demand, housing shortages are emerging more clearly, especially in large cities/metropolitan areas with a growing population. …
- Shortage contributes to increasing prices and rents.

The report goes on to discuss some of the differences in European countries:

> The most common tenure in Europe is owner occupation, with an average 69.4% of the population living in owner-occupied housing against 30.6% tenants. However, there are wide variations in tenure distribution across countries. Most former communist countries of Central and Eastern Europe show a very high share of home-owners without mortgage, as after the fall of the communist regimes, tenants were offered to buy the dwellings in which they lived at a low price. In Southern European countries outright ownership rates are also high. In most English-speaking and Nordic countries, Belgium and the Netherlands owners with outstanding mortgages are the most common tenure type. Only in Switzerland and Germany renting is more common than owning …

Housing is the highest expenditure item for households. Eleven percent of households are "overburdened" by housing costs as they spend over 40 percent of income on housing. The 2017 report also indicates that the share of poor people overburdened has increased from 35 percent in 2005 to over 39 percent in 2015. In Greece, Ireland, Portugal, and Spain, the housing cost overburden rate among the poor more than doubled over this period. Affordable housing policy across the European Union has been shifting away from having governments building housing to providing housing support to those with lower income levels, like housing vouchers in the United States. Thus, the construction of housing is primarily taking place in the private market.

Forecasts of housing demands in the European Union are much smaller than what is expected in other countries. Based on the United Nations' forecast, only about two million additional housing units will be needed by the year 2030. However, new housing in the coming years in the European Union will be provided in much the same fashion as in the US. Private development corporations will continue to provide housing for middle- and upper-income occupants. For low-income people, government assistance will largely be in the form of housing vouchers.

Housing in China

In China, construction of urban housing has been a major program of the central Chinese government. Again, in accordance with United Nations' forecast for population growth, it is estimated that China will have to build as many as fifty-five million new housing units between 2015 and 2030. The Chinese government announced in March 2011 the objective of building thirty-six million units of housing by 2015, a period of only four years.

Indeed, construction of new housing has been a major activity in China, as reported recently in Wikipedia:

> By 2014, Chinese builders have added 100 billion square feet of housing space in China, equating to 74 square feet per person. Construction of urban housing was a major undertaking. The country has shown a major shift in allocating funds and

resources to housing their people, building over 5.5 million apartments between the years of 2003 and 2014 in China's cities. These construction projects assigned by the state influence the construction job market in China as well. In 2014 alone, 29 million people were employed in urban construction businesses around China. (Wikipedia, from Glaeser 2017)

One downside to these programs is that some observers argue housing development is massively oversupplied and overvalued. In 2011, it was estimated that there were eighty-nine million empty apartments in China. Property analysts argue this is a bubble waiting to burst with serious consequences in the future. What is clear is that the government is attempting to meet the substantial rural-to-urban migration by having suitable vacant units available in the process. The building process is also oriented to much higher density than what is found in the United States.

The China housing program is a national government plan carried out by the government. The government hires the workers for each project and lays them off when the project is completed. Given the structure of the communist government, there appears to be little in the way of global corporate role. Given the propensity of growing megacities in China, more private businesses may come into being between now and 2050. As noted in chapter 2, China also has some of the world's largest banks, so funding the housing programs does not seem a likely problem.

Housing in India

Given the United Nations' projections, by 2030, India will need more than forty million new housing units, and close to sixty million new housing units between 2030 and 2050. As noted in chapter 2, by 2030, India will be leading the world along with China in the number of megacities—cities with more than ten million inhabitants. In 2030, India and China will both have seven of these huge urban areas. Thus, the two countries will have fourteen of the projected forty megacities in 2030.

India is a democracy with a long history of British control. Thus, the provision of housing is like that of the United Kingdom and the US. Most of the housing is built by private developers working with profit incentives in a market of private land ownership. However, to meet the needs of impoverished slum dwellers, the Indian government has developed publicly sponsored programs with substantial targets. The major challenge is that today, in 2018, India is seen as the most impoverished nation in the world.

The Jawaharlal Nehru National Urban Renewal Mission has built more than one million housing units for poor people living in slums. The program has been somewhat criticized for the locations of these units in relation to infrastructure and jobs. A more recent government program, the Pradhan Mantri Awas Yojana (PMAY), plans to provide homes to eighteen million households in urban India and nearly thirty million households in rural India.

Given its British heritage, the housing market in India is very much a private market. It does have problems arising from poor record keeping and distortions in the private market, such as owners of multiple housing units not offering them for rent or sale. In a society with great shortages of housing, this is a serious problem. Shreya Deb, in the *Hindu Business Line* (July 2017) reported the following:

> The Census showed there were over 10 million vacant houses in 2011, nearly half the urban housing shortage. The vast majority of these property owners are private citizens who prefer to leave their house vacant, rather than offer it on rent. This reflects the distorted rental market in India where property owners fear they may lose their property to tenants, leading to under-utilisation of assets.

According to the Deb article, additional significant challenges exist for India. One study showed that there was a shortage of close to nineteen million housing units in 2012. Yet there is an absence of capability to meet that shortage, notwithstanding the significant projected urban growth over the coming years. Another challenge cited is a lack of land needed for meeting housing shortages. Add to this the above-mentioned challenges for record keeping and the large numbers of vacant housing, and you have a picture of the significant problems India faces in housing its rapidly growing urban population.

Housing in Africa

Given the United Nations' predictions of population in Africa, my estimate is that from seventy to seventy-five million new housing units will be needed by 2030. The African population between 2030 and 2050 will grow even more, and in that period, there will be a likely need for 140 million additional housing units. Looking at the map in figure 2.4 in chapter 2, urban areas in Africa tend to show high rates of annual growth of 3 percent or more between 2018 and 2030. For 2018–2030, virtually all other cities in all other global continents will be growing at less than 3 percent per year. A World Bank report of 2015 estimates that sub–Saharan Africa is growing by 4.5 million residents each year.

Photograph by John Miller: Cape Town, South Africa, contrasting poor versus rich housing (https://www.millefoto.com/unequalscenesy73zav0gjcq1iibupgllgskm6x80jw).

Africa has already entered the throes of a housing crisis. Demand for decent housing far outstrips supply. African countries already have a high migration of population from rural to urban centers.

Looking at the larger African countries, consider first Egypt, with a population close to ninety million. The government is currently seeking to establish several housing projects to meet the existing housing deficit estimated conservatively at 3.5 million. In Nigeria, Africa's most populous country, the situation is not any better, with only one hundred thousand housing units being built annually, compared to an annual demand of seven hundred thousand, with an estimated present deficit of some seventeen million houses. In South

Africa, the government has built more than three million housing units on a subsidized basis since 1994. However, current estimates of the housing deficit stand at about two million. In East Africa, conditions in Kenya offer a similar picture. The 2013 Housing Survey by the Ministry of Lands and Housing in Kenya estimated the deficit at two million houses over the next ten years.

These statistics paint a grim picture of an ever-increasing deficit that will push more of Africa's population to slums and informal settlements, especially given the current population boom. Some African countries are showing signs of a growing economy, resulting in an increasing middle class. An African Development Bank report places the continent's middle-class population at 34.3 percent in 2010, far higher than the figure of 26.2 percent in 1980. The result is a rapid rise in urbanization, consumer spending, and higher housing expectations. The rate of urbanization is so high that UN-Habitat has estimated that forty thousand people move to cities in Africa every day.

Africa poses numerous problems for urbanization, as spelled out in a recent book by Jeffrey Sachs (2015). From the colonial legacy of the nineteenth century, there are forty-nine countries on the continent, the boundaries of which were settled primarily through colonial oversight from European countries. Sixteen of those countries are landlocked. Sachs also points out problems with unrealistic national boundaries, tropical weather conditions, difficult geography and topography, ongoing problems with malaria and other tropical diseases, and the lack of significant transportation facilities.

Thus, one could raise a question concerning the accuracy of the United Nations' forecasts for Africa. However, assuming the forecasts are correct, and given the continental problems, the question arises about the manner of providing affordable housing for Africa's rapidly growing population. Several socioeconomic factors are playing against the realization of this dream. Where there is a growing economy, land prices rise sharply along with the cost of building materials. Mortgage financing is very limited. Thus, new housing is increasingly becoming out of reach. Can there be a strong economy for the continent to absorb the rural-to-urban migration visualized? Will the continent attract global financial and construction interests? Clearly, the farthest northern and southern parts of the continent may realize growing urbanization in coming years. But the sub-Saharan countries, particularly those landlocked, face serious difficulties.

Alternative Building Technologies

One possibility for meeting future global housing needs lies in the promotion of prefabricated housing. This has been controversial for many years, as the technology emerged during World War II. Prefabricated homes were built in the US, the UK, and Sweden at that time.[40] Prefabricated housing has also been built in Australia and in Asia. This technology gives promise of quicker construction and higher quality, especially with greater insulation strength for meeting weather circumstances. This is accompanied by significantly lower costs. Controversy stems from a considerable reduction in the number of construction workers. The labor force is much smaller and is predominantly factory located.

Interestingly, a prefabricating firm is currently in business in South Africa. The firm is known as the Moladi Building Technology. This firm is being engaged to deliver 1.5 million new homes over a three-year period in that country. South Africa has completed several affordable housing projects using the Moladi Building Technology firm. This firm is also building housing in Nigeria. Other countries in Africa have also turned to prefabricated housing.[41]

In summary, I have focused on housing as it is clearly the most difficult problem facing the worldwide urban population growth, as forecast by the United Nations. Repeating the quote from Cédric Van Styvendael, is housing a basic human right or a business commodity? Globally, every country has had this challenge in its urban areas.

Future in Agriculture as It Affects Urbanization

The corporatist oligopoly in agriculture will be an important contributor to the urbanization process. The firms in this oligopoly produce seeds, herbicides, fungicides, insecticides, along with tractors and trucking equipment. They are also deeply involved in the new technology development described in

---

[40] My first owned house was prefabricated, built by Acorn Homes, in Massachusetts in 1963. It was the best insulated home I have ever lived in.

[41] Also working in Africa is International Green Structures, a prefabrication firm located in Maryland, USA.

chapter 5. The dominant firms already operate on a worldwide basis. Visiting their websites, one can immediately see that Monsanto has significant business in India and overall works in fifty countries. The merger of Dow and DuPont in 2017 converges their already substantial work in Africa as well as other countries. The firm Syngenta is the consolidation of many mergers in the twenty-first century. It too has operations in many countries around the world, as do Cargill and Archer Daniel Midlands. While Bayer is perhaps best known for over-the-counter medicine (aspirin), it is actively involved worldwide in agricultural technology and development. At this writing, the European Union has approved a merger of Monsanto and Bayer.

Some of these corporations have also been involved in worldwide controversies, particularly in terms of pricing, product yields, and environmental impacts. Each of the corporations is worth significantly more than billions of dollars, so these controversies can usually be accommodated, settled, and paid off. The companies are also involved in significant lobbying with governments that reputedly oversee their operations.

These companies operate on a worldwide basis, perhaps more than other oligopolies. In a positive sense, they are leaders in technological innovation for agriculture. With this activity, we may consider them to be assisting the urbanization process by creating safer and adequate food production while minimizing labor inputs necessary for that. One could also argue that by reducing labor inputs, they are encouraging rural to urban migration. As noted in the previous chapter, they are also severely challenged by environmental problems. However, they are clearly seeking to continue providing an adequate food supply for growing global populations (both rural and urban). Thus, in the long term, these companies may be very helpful in meeting the urbanization forecasts of the United Nations.

Communications

The rise of Google, Facebook, Comcast, and cell phone technology has had worldwide effects in a very short time. The oligopolies in this business are truly global. This can be seen in the recent concern with Facebook in conjunction with Cambridge Analytica intruding on the privacy of some eighty-seven million Facebook members. One of the largest corporations is Apple, the manufacturer of communications equipment. As previously noted, that company exists in many different countries around the world. Apple is of major concern, because they use countries with low labor costs to do the manufacturing of their computer and telephone products. Their creative, educated, and highly paid workforce designs the way communication technology works (predominantly in Silicon Valley). However, they are smaller in number compared to the uneducated, very low-paid foreign workers who actually make their physical products (computers, cell phones, etc.).

The cell phone is a dominant technological product being used throughout the world. India is reputed to be the nation with the largest number of users of cell phones in the world. Other countries, where landline phones have been either absent or not effective, are also now dominated by cell phones. This includes countries in Central and Eastern Europe and in Africa.

There is no question that communication technologies play a role of strong assistance in the urbanization process. Unfortunately, there is also clear evidence that global oligopolies will be dominant in this part of the urbanization process.

Commercial and Industrial Urban Land Development

The most important relationship of corporatism in land development is, of course, more focused on industrial and commercial development.[42] To be an urban area requires a basic economy; to be economically viable requires location in urban areas. From the 1950s to the present day, corporate interests in central business districts (CBDs) and in suburban industrial parks and commercial malls have been strong and influential, if not controlling.[43] In developed countries, today's CBDs are strongly dominated by banks, financial corporations, and Sassen's "producer services" (accounting, law, communications, credit, and other specialized services) (Sassen 2012, 5).

Concerning the corporate role in future urban development, assuming the increasing urban population forecasts, there is question as to how one might predict the role of corporatism in the future building of cities. The United Nations' forecasts show the urban growth taking place largely in Africa and Asia. There is little doubt that government will dominate in the planning of growing cities in China. This may

---

[42] Along with high cost luxurious housing.

[43] Before the 1950s many acres of central city land were industrial but as land requirements expanded, manufacturers moved away to suburbs or smaller cities.

also seem likely for urban growth in India, although global corporations could see a larger role in India. In Africa, opportunities for corporate ruling over urban development seem to be a significant possibility. Opportunities for corporate dominance seem to be evident, as corporate interests in land acquisition in Africa seem to be increasing. Also, land acquisition in Africa by the Chinese government has been increasing substantially.

Foreign land acquisition is usually oriented toward mining natural resources, such as oil, uranium, silver, and other natural chemicals and metals. Attention for this is usually not focused on urbanizing land but rather on land where costs are very low. Global corporations have been involved in this, but so have governments. Overall, it is difficult to predict the role of global corporate oligopolies in the coming urbanizing years. The economic sector that is most likely to be heavily involved is the global financial sector. The opportunities for global industry appear to be very favorable, given the low wages of the workforce living in these countries. The urbanization process would give rise both to factory workers and to newly enabled consumers.

Finally, there are oligopolistic corporations producing the raw materials essential to the building of urban development. The global influence of steel and aluminum production shows every tendency toward growth and expansion for existing firms and the probable decline of any local competition. Similarly, the energy oligopolies will likely see new urbanization as an opportunity for growth and dominance.

Government Incentives for Economic Development

One activity throughout the world is the process of offering incentives to bring global corporations toward a new nation. One of the key incentives in place for many decades now has been the availability of low-income labor costs. Historically, transportation costs were dominant in determining economic urbanity. Transportation costs have significantly declined. In the 1970s, American clothing manufacturers opened factories in Bangladesh and Latin America because labor costs were a tiny fraction of what they were in the United States. Thus, while transportation costs may have increased, the reduction of labor costs far offset such increases. For similar reasons, television manufacturers moved to Japan, South Korea, and other countries. Their technological innovations took place in the United States, but once routine factory operations were created, that led to massive production in countries with much lower labor costs.

Other types of incentives have also come into being, influencing the location of large corporations. These incentives are created by national or local governments and include the following:

- Overall low tax rate (in competition with other countries, cities, etc.). This has become a dominant incentive leading to corporate global establishment, as suggested in chapter 4.
- Tax deals (temporary or permanent; partial or full). This is also a common incentive that goes beyond the basic tax rate and suggests deals of tax payments independent of a national or state tax law. Some companies have been permanently exempted from any taxes. Some companies pay partial taxes either permanently or over a fixed time period.
- Loans. Some governments provide loans with very low interest rates and long periods of repayment.
- Land deals. Governments have used eminent domain to assemble a tract of land offered to a corporation at much lower cost (or even at no cost).

Use of these incentives has been analyzed thoroughly by Jensen and Malesky (2018), largely from the perspective of whether such incentives truly pay off the politicians of an urban area. They find extensive ineffectiveness of the use of incentives. One question remains: how do these incentives influence the urban labor force in terms of opportunity and stability?

The study of Jensen and Malesky (2018) involves not only international comparison analysis but also close analysis of the use of incentives by state and local governments in the United States. Their foremost case study focuses on Kansas City. This is a city with a dividing line in the center separating it into two states: the eastern part of the city is in Missouri, and the western part is in Kansas. From this, we can see firsthand substantial competition for incentives for economic locations in the two states, yet all within the same city.

Local governments in the United States are very much involved in offering competitive incentives to increase economic development in their urban areas. This occurs not only with incentives to foreign corporations but also to American corporations, with competition between states and between local governments in an urban region. Clearly, incentive is a technique used in the pursuit of corporate relocation activities.[44]

---

[44] As Jensen and Malesky (2018) point out, incentives can also work the other way. Since the development of incentives involves political and corporate leaders working together to set up a deal, there can also be corporate campaign contributions to the

One of the most publicized events starting in 2017 was the goal of the Amazon Corporation to create a second headquarters in addition to its Seattle home base. What was involved provided a clear illustration of today's premise of urban economic growth. Amazon was to hire fifty thousand workers and spend $5 billion in constructing its second headquarters. In choosing the city for this event, Amazon expected help from the selected city in paying for any new required infrastructure as well as a deal on local property or other taxes that might be entailed. In other words, the city that won Amazon's decision would face significant public expenditures and tax inducements.[45]

Public-Private Partnerships: Business-Government Collaboration

A key area of infrastructure provision lies in business-government collaboration that is known as public-private partnerships (PPP, 3P, P3). This is frequently used internationally as well as in the United States and Europe. The focus of a PPP usually deals with infrastructure that will be of integral benefit both to the private corporation and the general public.

PPP projects began in the late nineteenth and early twentieth centuries, primarily oriented to the urbanization process. Today, PPP projects are global. Thus, there are many projects in the United States, Canada, China, Russia, Japan, European countries, Latin America, and Australia. Investopedia explains it like this:

> Public-private partnerships between a government agency and private-sector company can be used to finance, build and operate projects, such as public transportation networks, parks and convention centers. Financing a project through a public-private partnership can allow a project to be completed sooner or make it a possibility in the first place. (Investopedia: https://www.investopedia.com/terms/p/public-private-partnerships.asp)

---

political leaders involved to maintain their continued public tenure.

[45] Amazon actually selected two sites, rather than one. Both were close to the residential properties of its CEO. After the selections were announced, local opposition first arose in the New York site, followed by local opposition in the Virginia site. Amazon has dropped the New York site.

PPPs are found in the development of railroad and transit systems, airports, bridges, tunnels, roads, parks, sports stadiums, and seaports. They have also been used in the provision of health services where a national government will partner with medical device firms, pharmaceutical firms, and health insurers. One unusual PPP project was an entire housing and mixed-use development involving 168 square kilometers near the city of Shantou in China. Similarly, the project in Toronto, Canada, mentioned earlier is another example of a PPP project.

These forms of partnership of government and business could well be important vehicles for handling increasing urban development, particularly in the provision of costly infrastructure. Social sustainable goals, however, will have to be fundamental. Business profits are obviously important in PPP contracts, as business engagement is usually significant, and profit is the dominant rationale for business engagement. But PPP contracts, given the current conditions in today's urban areas, will decidedly have to be oriented toward the UN sustainable goals of the coming decades.

Conclusion

This chapter has focused on the significant aspects of the urban development process and the potential institutional participation. Housing has been given dominant attention, as I see this as the most difficult area for the global urbanization process. Even today, in the poorest nations in the world, many people acquire housing by building it themselves, with the absence of water supply, sewage disposal, and mobility connections. In wealthier nations, urban areas have significant numbers of homeless people. Worldwide, adequate and affordable housing is one of the most difficult elements of the urbanization process.

It is clear, however, that global corporate interests will likely see significant opportunities in Asia, Africa, and many other countries, along with the continuing rise of opportunities in presently developed countries. The key problem is whether there can be honest regulation of global corporate oligopolies on a worldwide scale in the building of the forecasted urban communities. While housing may continue to be locally focused, agriculture, communications, credit, and other specialized services still have a strong possibility of expanded global, corporate oligopolies in the world's new urban centers.

It should be noted that local governments have become very concerned about global warming and climate change. This concern means that many cities around the world are conscious of the policies and plans they need for meeting global challenges. There are international organizations of cities with frequent international meetings to address contemporary issues. Two prominent organizations are C40 Cities, with ninety-six participating cities, and 100 Resilient Cities, with ninety-one participating cities.[46] Additional groups include Global Covenant of Mayors for Climate & Energy, Institute for Sustainable Communities, and International Institute for Sustainable Development. Another is the International Council for Local Environmental Initiatives (ICLEI). Many global cities are also participants in UN international conferences. Regional groups are also developing. In the United States, there is an organization known as Mississippi River Cities and Town Initiative. This organization involves local governments from Minnesota to Louisiana focused on environmental quality for the entire Mississippi River Valley.

---

[46] The organization 100 Resilient Cities was funded by the Rockefeller Foundation. Unfortunately, in April 2019, the foundation shut down its financial help.

One author who is very optimistic about the role of cities is Benjamin Barber:

> For neither sovereign states nor the international bodies built on their foundation can any longer provide a reliable foundation for human survival.
>
> Under these daunting conditions … cities alone offer real hope for democratic governance locally and globally. Only pragmatic problem solving by mayors who are neighbors and eminent excellent homeboys [homegirls] – mayors who are far more trusted than officials at higher levels of government – promises a sustainable *local* future. (Barber 2014, xi)

However, as Samuel Stein notes:

> …planners are committed to both securing social reproduction – or ensuring that people have the means to survive in the future – and to turning everyone's space into someone's profit. (Stein, 2019,16)

References

Barber, B. 2014. *If Mayors Ruled the World: Dysfunctional Nations, Rising Cities*. Paperback edition. New Haven: Yale University Press.

Boyd, B. 2017. "Urbanization and the Mass Movement of People to Cities." https://graylinegroup.com/urbanization-catalyst-overview/.

Brown, Peter. 2015. *How Real Estate Developers Think: Design, Profits, and Community*. Philadelphia: University of Pennsylvania Press.

Carliner, Michael, and Ella Marya. 2016. *Rental Housing: An International Comparison*. Cambridge, MA: Joint Center for Housing Studies of Harvard University.

Deb, S. 2017. "The Government Must Clear Policy Bottlenecks for the Pradhan Mantri Awas Yojana to Meet Its Ambitious Target." *Hindu Business Line*. https://www.thehindubusinessline.com/opinion/housing-for-all-theres-a-lot-to-be-built/article9756490.ece.

Glaeser, E. 2017. "A Real Estate Boom with Chinese Characteristics." *Journal of Economic Perspectives* 31:93. doi:10.1257/jep.31.1.93.

Harvey, David. 2010. *The Enigma of Capital: and the Crises of Capitalism*. New York: Oxford University Press.

Jensen, Nathan M., and E. J. Malesky. 2018. *Incentives to Pander: How Politicians Use Corporate Welfare for Political Gain*. Cambridge, UK: Cambridge University Press.

Pew Charitable Trust. 2018. "American Families Face a Growing Rent Burden." pewtrust.org.

Rodwin, L. 1956. *British New Towns Policy*. Cambridge, MA: Harvard University Press.

Sassen, S. 2012. *Cities in a World Economy*. 4th ed. Los Angeles: Pine Forge Press (Sage).

Skelcher, C. 2005. "Public-Private Partnerships and Hybridity." In the *Oxford Handbook of Public Management*. Edited by E. Ferlie, L. E. Lynn Jr., L. E. Lynn, and C. Pollitt. Oxford and New York: Oxford University Press. Chapter 15.

Stein, S. (2019). *Capital City: Gentrification and the Real Estate State*. London, New York: Verso Books.

"The State of Housing in the EU 2017." http://www.housingeurope.eu/resource-1000/the-state-of-housing-in-the-eu-2017.

Transparency International: Corruption Perceptions Index.

https://www.transparency.org/news/feature/corruption_perceptions_index_2017#table's.

United Nations Department of Economic and Social Affairs/Population Division. *World Urbanization Prospects: The 2014 Revision.*

Weiss, M. A. 1987. *The Rise of the Community Builders: The American Real Estate Industry and Urban Land Planning.* New York: Columbia University Press.

Chapter 7

Urban Planning Education for Overturning the Tragedy of the Commons

This [future] urbanisation increases the risk of uncontrolled chaos, poor management of urban social structures and unsustainable impacts on natural resources – particularly water and energy. This growth if it occurs within existing technologies, planning paradigms and organisational structures is likely to have a deleterious impact upon the quality of life of future human habitation on the Earth.

City foresight is critical for the survival of urban cultures as they have become the largest producers of entropy on the planet – threatening ecological, social and economic systems (e.g. climate change).

—Dr. Phillip Daffara, Queensland, Australia (https://www.linkedin.com/pulse/so-newnew-urban-agenda-dr-phillip-daffara/)

The global and local trends outlined in the preceding chapters suggest serious challenges for the next decade and beyond, especially for the sustainability planning of growing urban areas. The UN forecasts the world urban population will become 6.6 billion by 2050, so urban planning becomes a highly significant undertaking, especially given the present-day Tragedy of the Commons. If we are to overcome this tragedy, one key intimation is the need for broader **urban** transdisciplinary knowledge, design, and leadership.

Urban planning education today is small in scale and still strongly influenced by architecture and landscape architecture. A 2013 study of urban planning faculty in the US showed that faculty interests were still dominated by physical urban design (Sanchez and Afzalan 2014). These are important skills, but they are not wholly adequate in urban planning.

Professional education in American universities has primarily focused on law, medicine, education, and business.[47] Graduate urban planning education is very small in comparison. In the United States there are currently 254 law schools and 175 medical schools, compared to seventy-two graduate planning schools (master's level; thirty-two baccalaureate). With close to six billion people occupying urban areas by 2030, there needs to be more concentration on appropriate education for urban planning.[48]

Historic urban areas have been a primary source of destructive climate behavior. To overcome the Tragedy of the Commons and create future urbanity that meets all of the UN's seventeen sustainable goals is a primary focus for urban planning. Meeting the UN's seventeen sustainable goals requires going beyond architecture, urban design, and infrastructure engineering.

The challenge for a professional urban planner includes a full understanding of how to deal with urban growth, corporate and oligopolistic urban economics, achieving quality, comprehensive and adequately compensated labor forces, designing effective governmental institutions, enhancing social psychology, health and education, community engagement, and designing means to diminish or eliminate urban crime. In

---

[47] There are 831 academic business institutions in fifty-four countries and territories that have earned AACSB accreditation. Similarly, 187 institutions hold an additional, specialized AACSB accreditation for their accounting programs (https://www.google.com/search?client=firefox-b-1-d&q=number+of+business+schools+in+the+US).

[48] From internet exploration, globally there are 553 planning schools, with 913 law schools and 2,753 medical schools. Globally, urban planning is still a minor educational focus.

the twentieth century, urban planning developed a strong orientation to citizen participation. Today, urban planning needs to not only include leadership of citizen participation but also a strong ability to lead in transdisciplinary understanding. Included, as well, is capability in taking advantage of growing technology in artificial intelligence.

The goal of this chapter is to provide a broad-scale answer to the question, what are the future training demands for urban planning? What are the additional curriculum needs that would justify expanding the urban planning graduate training program to be formed as a full, independent, transdisciplinary college?

Universities should consider creating an academic urban planning enterprise that is on the same level as medicine, law, education, and business. The enterprise should be focused on the growing needs of the global expanding urban population. The approach must include broader, more detailed environmental planning, a new approach to urban economics, and more expansive social, psychological, institutional, legal, and political aspects of urban planning activity. The problems outlined in the previous chapters need much closer attention in urban planning education.

In the United States, the Planning Accreditation Board provides the curriculum requirements for US accreditation that are quoted in box 7.1. The requirements are itemized in considerable generality. One can also note that environmental problems are not even mentioned. A planning program can be accredited even if one or more of the requirements are provided only in a very limited sense.[49] There is great variability among the seventy-two programs in the United States. Some continue to emphasize traditional linkages with architecture and landscape architecture, with great attention focused on physical design (these tend to be located within schools of architecture).[49]

---

[49] For example, many schools combine planning theory and planning history into a single one-semester course. In recent years, planning theory has become increasingly elaborate, multipronged, and philosophically deep. Thus, in a single semester, a student would not really achieve a full sense of either history or theory. A recent study unfortunately suggested that very few planning faculties are primarily interested in either one (Sanchez and Afzalan 2013).

Box 7.1. Planning Accreditation Board curriculum requirements

"1) *General Planning Knowledge*: The comprehension, representation, and use of ideas and information in the planning field, including appropriate perspectives from history, social science, and design and other allied fields.

a) Purpose and Meaning of Planning: why planning is undertaken by communities, cities, regions, and nations, and the impact planning is expected to have.

b) Planning Theory: behaviors and structures available to bring about sound planning outcomes.

c) Planning Law: legal and institutional contexts within which planning occurs.

d) Human Settlements and History of Planning: growth and development of places over time and across space.

e) The Future: relationships between past, present, and future in planning domains, as well as the potential for methods of design, analysis, and intervention to influence the future.

f) Global Dimensions of Planning: interactions, flows of people and materials, cultures, and differing approaches to planning across world regions.

2) *Planning Skills*: The use and application of knowledge to perform specific tasks required in the practice of planning.

a) Research: tools for assembling and analyzing ideas and information from prior practice and scholarship, and from primary and secondary sources.

b) Written, Oral and Graphic Communication: ability to prepare clear, accurate and compelling text, graphics and maps for use in documents and presentations.

c) Quantitative and Qualitative Methods: data collection, analysis and modeling tools for forecasting, policy analysis, and design of projects and plans.

d) Plan Creation and Implementation: integrative tools useful for sound plan formulation, adoption, and implementation and enforcement.

e) Planning Process Methods: tools for stakeholder involvement, community engagement, and working with diverse communities.

f) Leadership: tools for attention, formation, strategic decision-making, team building, and organizational/community motivation.

3) *Values and Ethics*: Values inform ethical and normative principles used to guide planning in a democratic society. The Program shall incorporate values and ethics into required courses of the curriculum, including:

a) Professional Ethics and Responsibility: key issues of planning ethics and related questions of the ethics of public decision-making, research, and client representation (including the provisions of the AICP Code of Ethics and Professional Conduct, and APA's Ethical Principles in Planning).

b) Equity, Diversity and Social Justice: key issues in equity, diversity, and social justice that emphasize planners' role in expanding choice and opportunity for all persons, plan for the needs of the disadvantaged, reduce inequities through critical examination of past and current systems and disparities, and promote racial and economic integration.

c) Governance and Participation: the roles of officials, stakeholders, and community members in planned change.

d) Sustainability and Environmental Quality: environmental, economic, and social/political factors that contribute to sustainable communities, and the creation of sustainable futures.

e) Growth and Development: economic, infrastructure, social, and cultural factors in urban and regional growth and change.

f) Health and Built Environment: planning's implications on individual and community health in the places where people live, work, play and learn.

B. Areas of Specialization and Electives: The Program shall have sufficient depth in its curriculum and faculty in the specialization areas and electives it offers to assure a credible and high quality offering.

1) *Specializations*: When a program includes specialization fields, it is assumed that they are built on top of the general planning foundation and that courses in the areas of specialization add significantly to the basic planning knowledge, skills and values. Programs must demonstrate that there are enough courses in the areas of specialization that students get the depth and range of materials to give them a level of expertise.

2) *Electives*: The curriculum shall contain opportunities for students to explore other areas such as exposure to other professions, other specializations, and emerging trends and issues."

Those located in schools of public administration or public policy tend to provide more attention to social science and quantitative methods of analysis, along with focus on the institutional, legal, and political aspects of urban planning activity. Emphasis also tends to be in traditional urban economics, political science, and, to a limited extent, sociology. The problems outlined in the previous chapters need much closer attention in urban planning education.

Given the expansive nature of urban life today and in coming years, the fundamental curriculum in urban training needs to be expanded from four semesters to at least six, with added coursework, research, and internships in global climate impacts on urban areas, global economic impacts, trends in political authoritarianism, and the problems of social ecology and human interaction within all these milieus. The new independent college additionally needs to create a truly transdisciplinary faculty. This leads to the necessity for an enlarged independent college, equal in size and greater in transdisciplinary resources than medicine, law, education, and business.[50]

I was fortunate to find a diagram on the website of the Boston Consulting Group (https://www.bcg.com/).[51] They produced a diagram showing ten dimensions of well-being involved in a sustainable, economic-development process. This diagram struck me as an excellent beginning portrayal of the full curriculum for contemporary urban planning education (figure 7.1). Many sectors in the ten-sector diagram have been omitted historically in urban planning education, especially by those programs that are still primarily focused on architecture.

This diagram suggests not a hierarchy of curriculum needs but rather areas of equal priority and attention. Discussion, however, will begin at the top. Below, issues expanding on the sectors of figure 7.1 will be explored as follows:

A. Environmental Planning
B. Urban Economics (including income and income inequality, stability, and employment)
C. Future Social Investment (health and mental health, education, infrastructure)
D. Sustainability (housing accessibility, social cohesion, racial and gender equality, safety, trust, government effectiveness)

---

[50] Two universities have programs that approach these requirements, Arizona State University and the University of California, Irvine.

[51] The Boston Consulting Group is a consulting firm with ninety locations in fifty countries.

Figure 7.1. An illustrative full curriculum for urban planning

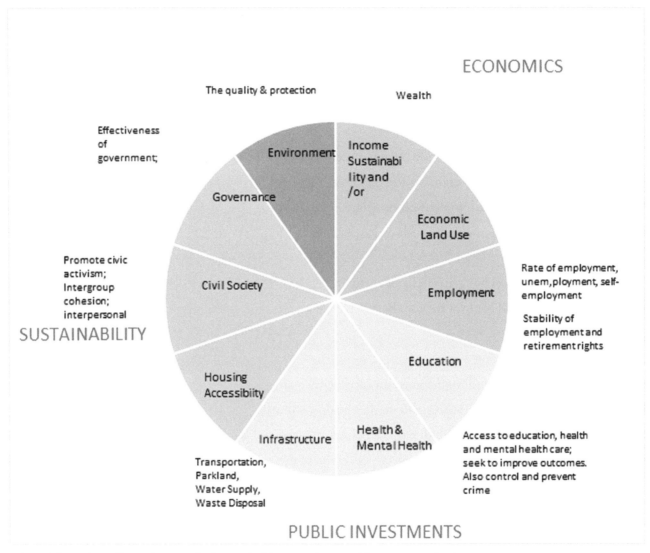

Adapted from: https://www.bcg.com/industries/public-sector/sustainable-economic-development-assessment.aspx

The two sectors labeled Governance and Civil Society tend to be areas where planning education provides variable and limited focus. After graduation, planning students tend to work in local governments but seldom challenge the institutional framework that those governments possess or their history of success or accountability.

While this diagram in figure 7.1 can be considered a basic framework for urban planning education, there are also deeper concerns that need to be well thought out. Each of the ten sectors in the diagram are generalities where each requires great depth of study. For example, in health, there also needs to be stronger and deeper concern for factors relating to mental health.

Attention also needs to be paid to the interaction between and among the sectors. Clearly, as we have seen in chapters 3 and 4, there can be significant struggle between economics and governance. Obviously, the economic sector has serious implications for both environmental quality and income inequality.

Many writers have argued that what we really have is a need for multidisciplinary team efforts. One author has argued for what he calls "social ecology" exploring human and environmental interactions, along with human-to-human interactions (Stokols 2018). These disciplines are not generally included in the education of an urban planner, yet they are essential in any urban planning effort. These include interdisciplinary work from psychology, anthropology, behavioral economics, and ecological economics. While planning programs today may pay attention to urban economics, politics, and sociology, it is not always conclusive how these fields will solve serious urban problems such as poverty, racial segregation, urban crime, health, and mental health, along with environmental issues.

The infrastructure sector has clear relations with governance, urban economics, and the quality of the environment. Moreover, the infrastructure sector offers opportunities for significant improvements by advancing skills in the energy and communications technologies. One important outline of this can be seen in the recent book by Jeremy Rifkin, *The Third Industrialization Revolution* (Rifkin 2010). New technology may have negative effects on labor force and inequality, but it also shows promise for aiding better prospects for energy, land use, transportation, and residential development.

Figure 7.1 is really a generalization of the scope of education for urban planners. It points out the broad scope of the transdisciplinary necessity of future urban planning education. My overview of an approach to future urban planning has been strongly influenced by a book by Daniel Stokols: *Social Ecology in the Digital Age: Solving Complex Problems in a Globalized World* (Stokols 2018). This book describes a growing area of scholarship and research and, in many ways, reflects a growing trend toward multidisciplinary teamwork. The last decade has seen several excellent books published with this in mind. The many disciplines involved include psychology, social psychology, anthropology, economic behaviorism, ecological economics, and others.

Stokols, who teaches at the School of Social Ecology at the University of California, Irvine, provides one of the best descriptions of how to proceed. In his book, he focuses on the integration of social and behavioral sciences with environmental science and virtual innovation. He describes the characteristic activities that he is promoting as social ecology.

> Social ecology, for example, is not a discipline in its own right but rather a cross-disciplinary framework that integrates concepts and methods from different fields to achieve a broader understanding of complex problems within particular *spatial, temporal, sociocultural, and virtual (cyber-mediated) contexts.* (Stokols 2018, 323) (Emphasis added.)

He criticizes multidisciplinary efforts where the scholars work independently within their own fields while engaging in occasional part-time internet collaboration with others in different fields. His approach emphasizes collaborative team activities:

> In *transdisciplinary* collaborations, scholars from different fields collaborate closely over extended periods to create novel conceptual and methodological frameworks that not only integrate *but also transcend their respective disciplinary perspectives.* (Stokols 2018, 323) (My emphasis.)

This transdisciplinary approach is what is required in future urban planning. Urban planning scholars are beginning to see the need for more integrated social, economic, and environmental understanding of the major trends that I have outlined here. In our contemporary world, we do have problems of mental health, and it is an important question as to what extent urban environments are creating the conditions for generating adverse mental health. We have problems of poverty, racial and foreign segregation, religious hate, and crime, all of which create mental health pressures on those regularly experiencing such difficulties. If these problems are to be solved or at least diminished by 2050, at the time when two-thirds of the world population are forecast to be urban, we need the transdisciplinary approach. Individual scholarly fields cannot answer the interconnecting physical and social problems.

A. Expansion of Environmental-Planning Knowledge and Skill

As stated by Ian Gough, "Climate change threatens human well-being across the world and into the future" (Gough 2017, 19). It has been described as a "truly complex and diabolical policy problem." Thus, it is apparent that a person skilled in urban planning needs full recognition of climate and environmental impacts.

This can be fundamentally illustrated by the activity of developing even a single building, as I noted at the end of chapter 2. Impacts of climate and environmental features that are destroyed (or possibly enhanced) in creating land for a new building need to be foreseen, along with the environmental impacts of the construction process. There needs to follow analysis of the impacts of climate and environmental features that are destroyed (or helped) as people occupy and carry out activities in the building (residential, commercial, industrial, recreational) or engage in transportation to or from the building. Attention needs to be paid to consumption and demand for water and waste. This analysis should be focused on immediate environmental and climate consequences as well as forecasting future impacts.

This applies to any new building or a set of new buildings (such as a neighborhood housing development, an industrial park, a downtown office skyscraper, a shopping mall, a sports stadium, or neighborhood alteration). This also applies to efforts at building or improving infrastructure facilities or restoring earth features such as woodland, topography, or water resources.

In addition, a critical area of research and understanding is the notion of human activities and their climate effects. For example, there are research findings indicating that the wealthier human beings are, the more they contribute to global warming (Gough 2017). People purchasing SUVs and using them only for single-driver basic commuting to work, shopping, and recreation (rather than truck work) are an example of a needless contribution to global warming. Urban planners need to work carefully around deeper issues, such as inequality, that impact climate change or environmental resources in any process of designing new urban capacities.

Most planning programs today do teach about concerns of earth resources. Indeed, the latest PAB curriculum standard (2017, 1f) even argues planning education should incorporate "Global Dimensions of Planning: interactions, flows of people and materials, cultures, and differing approaches to planning across world regions." While a new standard, it is still quite general and nonspecific, but it leads in the right direction (note, however, that the word "environment" does not appear in the new standard).

There is ongoing science about how urban development affects global warming and its impacts on ocean levels, ocean acidification, nitrogen levels, phosphorus levels, and so forth. The research in this area tends to focus on global scales. However, the impacts do occur at the local level (as in Houston, Puerto Rico, and Paris in 2017–2018; Florida, Mexico, and Indonesia in 2018). Planners at the local level need to develop research and understanding of these local issues. While the global population growth may, as forecasted, be 2.5 billion people, global environmental impacts occur in each individual urban area. The planning of a specific urban area needs to account for how that area may be furthering climate change and environmental destruction and how these problems can be solved.

Many consumer choices that have significant deleterious climate and environmental impacts are understood as temporary and transitory. However, this requires an area of urban planning research that is currently quite limited. Clearly, when we drive our car, there are climate and environmental impacts.[52] How we dispose of waste has significant climate and environmental impacts.[53] Heating and cooling our homes have climate and

---

[52] An op-ed piece in my local newspaper from an opponent to the city's planning department included the following: "we are a gas guzzling people and love driving our big cars alone."

[53] Also, in my local newspaper (March 23, 2018) was a story with a headline reading "Collection of ocean garbage now twice the size of Texas." The article notes that ocean plastic garbage is growing at an exponential rate. Recently published by the journal *Scientific Reports*, it deals with the Pacific Ocean between California and Hawaii. The garbage consists largely of plastic consumer waste products.

environmental impacts. Even grilling a steak in a suburban backyard has climate and environmental impacts. In the planning of growing and new urban areas, there is need for much more fundamental and deep concern for the climate and environmental impacts of our planning proposals.

B. The Urban Economy

The global corporatist oligopolistic framework as described in chapter 3 dominates the urban economy of today.[54] The ever-increasing global pursuit of both greed and power (profit and control) by oligopolistic-corporate leadership gives us a new perception of what urban economics is about and what is likely to emerge as the global urban population grows. This issue is not simply about global economics; it has serious impacts on local urban areas, including impacts on technology, manufacturing, worker skills and education, labor force well-being, and social and physical stability (and of course climate and environmental impacts).

---

[54] Including domination of land, land value and land use (Stein, 2019)

I live in an urban area that has many global corporations. We are lucky in that these corporations are very prosperous and have historically had strong philanthropic tendencies. However, one of our significantly important corporations recently moved its headquarters to Ireland. As noted in chapter 3, this provides the firm with a much lower tax rate (even lower than the tax law passed in the US in December 2017). It also provided an opportunity for a merger and acquisition without regulatory antitrust oversight. The question for those of us living in my urban area is, what will be the effect of this form of global economics on our local economy? At the time of the relocation, we were assured that the local manufacturing factory and its labor force would remain the same. It still raises the question, however, of the future effects on the local economy. With lower labor costs (along with lower taxes) in the new foreign headquarters, we in our urban area clearly need to have some concern about the future local employment impact of this global move.

An even more difficult experience with corporatism is found in the city of New London, Connecticut. The city's neighborhood of Fort Trumbull had old single- and multifamily homes built in the early twentieth century. The city government took possession of the entire neighborhood through the process of eminent domain and demolished the housing in 2000 as part of an economic development plan. Local homeowners, including Susette Kelo, challenged the eminent domain act because her property was being seized for private use rather than public use. On February 22, 2005, the US Supreme Court ruled on the case of *Kelo v. City of New London*. In a 5–4 vote, the court ruled that the city may seize privately owned property under eminent domain and that it could subsequently be used for *private* economic development. Despite the city's legal victory, the development plan never got off the ground. The private redeveloper was to be the Pfizer Corporation, a key member of the pharmaceutical oligopoly noted in chapter 3.

Pfizer decided to move to another city, and the New London land taken by eminent domain has remained vacant as of this writing in 2019. One may question the viability of the city's planning for this neighborhood. They clearly were following the US law that underlay urban redevelopment activities in the 1950s but had pretty much been discontinued by most American urban areas by the 1970s. Whether the plan was good or bad, obviously the city was damaged by the changed location decision of the global corporation. In effect, oligopolistic corporations (including real estate corporations) can have significant control over economic and government institutions at the local level—some of which can be very profitable and some of which, as experienced by the city of New London, can be extraordinarily damaging.

A new project involves an international Chinese corporation that scheduled to build a new factory in eastern Wisconsin, on Interstate I-94 a few miles south of Milwaukee. The initial plan was announced in 2017. The company's name is Foxconn. The company would invest $10 billion in a new plant and hire thirteen thousand workers. They would receive $4 billion in tax breaks and other subsidies over the next fifteen years from the state. They would be producing high-tech liquid-crystal display screens. After public relations with the state governor and the US president, Foxconn has since backed down, and at this writing, it is not clear exactly how the project will move forward. In the age of giant corporations, urban economic planning today can be more difficult and very different from traditional ways of planning.

The traditional teaching of urban economics in planning schools has largely followed a longtime local focus with theories going back to Alfred Weber and the importance of transportation costs, to the microeconomic theories of <u>Alonso</u>, <u>Christaller</u>, and <u>Lösch.</u> These tended to be spatial, geographic orientations, with focus on determining how economic functions determine land value (and how land value determines land use). In addition, scholars also made the distinction between economic activity that was exporting goods or services and those that were purely offering local business activity. Regional Economist Walter Isard took the input-output methods of Leontief and applied them to regional economic interaction that gave strong analysis for the exporting of goods. Another important contribution was Paul Krugman's study of economic geography, for which he earned a Nobel Prize in economics. Michael Porter, of the Harvard Business School, has also made important contributions on economic firm geographical clustering and competition.

Clearly, a city without an economy is not a city. Cities do not develop and evolve without the location decisions of business firms—decisions clearly linked to the forces in the specific market area and that depend on economic geography. These forces tend to have effects on clustering of economic activity in an urban area and tends to affect the size of the urban area and its demand for labor, infrastructure, housing, and consumer services. Research in these phenomena help the urban economist explain why cities develop where they do, why cities are large or small, what causes economic growth and decline, and how local governments affect urban growth.

Three new books recently published, however, begin to give greater attention to the global character of urban economics. These include Philip McCann's (2013) *Modern Urban and Regional Economics*, second edition (Oxford, UK: Oxford University Press) (especially his final section) and Sasaki Sassen's (2012) *Cities in a World Economy*, fourth edition (Los Angeles: Pine Forge Press). The third book is a collection of essays edited by three British authors, *A Research Agenda for Regeneration Economies*. They are very important readings for urban planners.

Additional contemporary contributors include Richard Florida and Enrico Moretti. Florida's work is important in that he has shown that continued prosperity of an individual urban economy is very much dependent upon innovation and creativity, usually in an area dominated by major universities. This is highlighted in his most recent work, *The New Urban Crisis* (also in his earlier work, *The Rise of the Creative Class*). The San Francisco area and Silicon Valley have had their growth primarily arising from the University of California, Berkeley and Stanford University. Other cities noted in Florida's work included Seattle, Boston, New York, and Washington, DC, all of which have major universities. Florida illustrates lack of innovation and creativity with today's US Rust Belt.

Moretti's recent book, *The New Geography of Jobs*, also emphasizes the importance of creative and innovative forces. Another interesting example is the city of Pittsburgh, as noted in chapter 4. Once the center of steel production, the city became part of the Rust Belt. However, Pittsburgh has returned to some level of prosperity thanks to efforts by the Carnegie Mellon Institute, the University of Pittsburgh, and the Westinghouse and Bechtel Corporations. Pittsburgh today is viewed as an important center of robotic innovation (Katz and Nowak 2017).

Today, urban planning education should include ecological economists (Herman Daly, Robert Ayres, Tim Jackson). Ecological economists pay primary attention to the concepts of economic stability versus economic growth. Their orientations are primarily national or international with inclusion of environmental concerns. Clearly, however, ecological economics also involves local urban areas. Urban economic stability needs to be a major focus of urban economic development, including attention to worker health and well-being. This is particularly the case in manufacturing, where global pursuit of international low-wage workers is paramount (along with robotic machinery), creating the Rust Belt urban areas in the United States. Thus, there is the continued need for attending to economic geography and especially a new interlocking of economic and environmental geography.

Urban economic development in the age of global, oligopolistic corporatism is a fundamental concern for urban population expansion over the next twenty to thirty years. It is also of concern in relationship with government. There is a present-day dominance over national governments (and in the United States over many state governments). At the level of local urbanity, there are difficult challenges for urban planners. Cities like Pittsburgh can grow, despite losing corporate leadership in a key area of the economy, by use of innovations (especially with the help of two universities). A city like New London or other smaller Rust Belt cities can experience serious decline.

The urban economy of the twenty-first century is a volatile phenomenon. People trained as urban economic planners need to have a deep understanding and strategy for dealing with high uncertainty created by global oligopolistic corporatism. Clearly, urban economies today are dependent upon creativity and innovation, as explored by Florida and Moretti. On the other hand, the creative urban economies of today are vulnerable to innovations having significant deleterious effects on the local labor force. Creativity and innovation rely on requirements of education and skill. Those lacking education and skill are increasingly becoming serious problems in terms of low-wage service employment, unemployment, and poverty. Inequality is a growing urban problem. As Florida points out, this is not restricted to Rust Belt cities; it is also a serious problem for the cities that are creatively growing. They are experiencing major increases in housing costs and resulting gentrification. How this works out in a growing urban population is a fundamental question for the training of professional urban planners.

Creative ideas for reform of the oligopolistic-corporatist economy may have their beginnings in a book by Hill and Painter, *Better Bankers, Better Banks* (2015). The first part of their book describes the many disturbing practices (some illegal) carried out by banks in the period between 2010 and 2015 (the period just following the Great Recession). The second part of the book argues for regulation that would seriously curtail such scandals. As they put it, "certainly much bank behavior is not problematic. But the behavior [inappropriate or illegal] we discussed here is sufficiently common that cannot fairly be considered exceptional or rare" (Kindle location 350–55).

Hill and Painter go on to point out:

> A New York Times analysis of enforcement actions during the last 15 years found at least 51 cases in which 19 Wall Street firms had broken antifraud laws they had agreed never to break. (Kindle location 375, from Wyatt, *New York Times*, "Promises Made, and Remade, by Firms in S.E.C. Fraud Cases," November 7, 2011)

Going back to chapter 3, I reported on 136 violations of the Foreign Corrupt Practices Act (FCPA) between 2000 and 2016, involving not only banks but also a wide variety of top foreign and US corporations. Also, in chapter 3 is data concerning how corporations work to avoid paying taxes.

Clearly, the dominance of the oligopolistic-corporatist economy, including its increasing control over governments and labor unions, provides significant and challenging implications for urban planning. The traditional literature on urban economics simply has not addressed these problems. Research and scholarship (and education) in the field of urban economics needs to be significantly expanded—including, where possible, joint activities with business and education schools. Planners could also be an integral part of searching for positive alternatives to today's neoliberal economic theory.

Overall, today's global economic system is a deep fundamental challenge to the problems of urban growth, development, and sustainability. Today's economy is steered not only by Adam Smith's psychological pursuit of greed but also the psychology of ruling power, as noted in chapter 4. The oligopolistic-corporatist economy has paid almost no attention to its impact on the health of the planet Earth. It radiates power over governance institutions. It views human labor as mere production devices and replaceable by robots or other machines. Thus, for urban planning, the oligopolistic-corporatist economy is probably one of the top trials for stabilization of the comprehensive human needs of any local urban area. Andres and Bryson pointed out the following:

> All city-regions are connected to the global economy, but in very different ways. Some are directly involved in contributing to shaping the ongoing evolution of globalization. Others are more peripheral while possibly being shaped by decisions going on elsewhere. Some are small, middle sized, or large city-regions. (Andres and Byson 2018, chapter 1)

The noted economist Jeffrey Sachs gives us perhaps the top question of the day:

> And what happens when the world economy is on a collision course with the physical environment? Is there a way to change course, a way to combine economic development with environmental sustainability? (Sachs 2015, 3)

This truly promises to be one of the most difficult challenges for the urban planning profession. The combination of corporate dominance and antienvironmental behavior needs to be challenged extensively and effectively in urban planning practice. Economic dominance in effect extends right down to each and every land parcel – clearly an urban planning struggle.

As Samuel Stein points out:

> As long as land and buildings are bought and sold in a private market, there can be no truly democratic control over the city. (Stein, 2019, 195)

C. A Broader, Interdisciplinary Approach to Urban Planning Education

A key concern is exactly how we approach the problems of a significantly expanding urban population, a growing, powerful, world corporatist economy, and the rapidly growing, complex climate and environmental endangerment. How do deep global problems affect the future of local urban regions? Moreover, how do we develop the knowledge to tackle and solve these problems? Many of these problems already exist today and likely will grow worse in the future. With no success at finding broad solutions, we can expect a global expansion of poverty and serious consequences for urban health, mental health, education, employment opportunities, crime, and social unrest.[55] Growing world inequality will lead to more serious hindrances to effective urban life, together with severe environmental problems.

For at least three decades, there has been an emerging interdisciplinary area of research linking urban life and climate and environmental complications. There has been concern with the urban areas, but there appears to be little linkage of this new research to programs that train urban planners. This scholarly, broad, interdisciplinary approach to research and decision-making is essential to the education of planners, given all the trends and potentials outlined in my previous chapters.

---

[55] Current political activity requires that I also include a potential for future war and terrorism. As happened in the past few years, it is also apparent that war and terrorism are increasingly an urban problem.

I was a graduate student in the 1950s. In the city where I studied, there were serious problems of racial segregation, poverty, and crime. Obviously, these problems are still prominent today, not only in the city where I studied but also with virtually all global urban areas. The forecast for future urban population suggests the need for greater attention to finding solutions to these problems. Thus, an important area for urban planning education is broader and deeper interdisciplinary research.

The diagram sectors on figure 7.1, governance and civil society, are not fully covered in planning curricula. Within civil society, some planning programs have developed joint programs with schools of public health, schools of law, and engineering schools. However, there does tend to be an absence of concern with mental health, a significant factor in urban crime and other urban social and psychological problems. Some programs do pay attention to education but primarily making forecasts of public enrollment while having too little concern for educational quality or for racial or poverty troubles in public education.[56] These of course are of critical concern in an urban area's future.

Recent journal publications suggest that some planners are indeed concerned about the civil society sector. Issues of social cohesion, trust, racial equality, gender equality, crime, and safety are increasingly being talked about in professional journals, but such discussions mainly focus on the existence of these problems, with only limited attention to the possible means of alleviating them.

Planners have been concerned about housing since the beginning of the profession. Using legal tools of zoning and subdivision control, housing policies reflect desirable housing goals. However, in the United States, the actual construction of housing accommodation is primarily left to real estate corporations (occasionally helped by architects) who also draw upon the banking, finance, and insurance sectors. In the United States, public housing had a period in the Roosevelt years and in post–World War II years. Today, there is greater concentration on vouchers and similar limited programs, based on agreements with private owners.

As noted in chapter 6, the US has high rates of people living with rent "burdens," defined as paying rents more than 30 percent of income (including many paying rents greater than 50 percent of income). Countries in Europe also show high numbers of families with rent burdens. In countries not equipped to deal with

---

[56] In the twenty-first century, a key educational problem is safety. Mass shootings in a public high school have become more and more common.

housing, one can find many acres of land filled with self-built sheds, with limited or no public services, particularly in Africa, Southeast Asia, and Latin America. Public housing is still important in other countries. The United Kingdom has had a strong historic interest in public housing, which is still part of the tradition of India and other countries formerly ruled by the UK. China is also a strong provider of public housing.

Planners are educated about governance. However, the focus is largely on local governance since this is the primary problem orientation for newly trained planners starting their professional career. In the United States, local governments focus on land-use control. Also, in the United States, however, there are three levels of governance.

The highest level is dominated by corporate control, creating the dynamics of local urban economies described above. On the state level, corporate control is prevalent in a majority of state governments. This is an arena of significant governance interaction with local government. Interrelations of all levels of governance is vital in urban planning education.

In addition, however, is the issue of governance change—the manner and means of bringing about significant improvement in governance. Governance at all levels has contributed insufficiently in providing the means of eliminating racial segregation, poverty, poor housing, and unemployment. Urban crime is required to be identified, but urban crime rates persist, especially in neighborhood areas with segregation and poverty (many cities have pointed to decreasing crime rates, yet there are still significant cases of crime).

As suggested in chapter 6, housing problems are global. Yet also global are problems of poverty, crime, segregation, and discrimination. The countries of Scandinavia are perhaps the only global center where these problems exist at very low levels, including their urban centers.

All these institutional levels are felt in urban land use planning worldwide, right down to physical parcel levels.

D. The Process of Design

Given the historical emergence from architecture, the field of urban planning has always paid attention to the design process. However, that orientation toward design is primarily focused on physical design. Thus, planners have gone beyond individual buildings and engaged in designing street patterns, parklands, neighborhoods, shopping malls, industrial parks, and water and waste infrastructure. The focus is on how all these physical features are spatially/

geographically laid out. However, what is not taken up is the design of social and institutional patterns. We need to design not only *things*; we also need to design *relationships* and *human experiences*.

Once a problem has been identified and its multicausal dynamics are seen, there remains the key question, what is to be done? How to answer this question is the essence of planning, as I noted in a previous publication:

> It is important to note at the outset that this movement is essentially normative and speculative. It is normative in the sense that every effort in planning involves desires— whether it is a plan for a social gathering … or a plan for redeveloping a neighborhood or urban center. Being normative, it is an effort to improve circumstances—making things better than what they presently are. Thus, a plan is a collection of values involving aesthetic sensibilities, idealized social and economic relations, greater efficiencies/ convenience, or an advanced sense of self. (Bolan 2017, 240)

In short, in deciding what is to be done, chosen actions are focused on the way things *ought to be*.

One person, not an academic scholar, has shown significant skill in social design. Tim Brown is the CEO of a consulting firm that specializes in helping business firms develop their organizational design—combinations of hierarchical and working team patterns. He is not impressed by bureaucratic hierarchy but sees organizational design as focused on human relationships and experience.

As I summarized in my previous publication:

> In an intellectual sense, [design] calls upon the full range of human mental capacities—simultaneously requiring both a sophisticated synthetic awareness and an understanding of existing circumstances together with an imaginative conception of possible future circumstances. Understanding and explanation are necessary but insufficient conditions for creating *normative* visions of future possibilities and imagining the actions that can realize the best of those possibilities. (Bolan 2017, 254) (Emphasis added.)

Finally, the contemporary notion of designing today needs to be more and more oriented toward collaborative teamwork.

Thus, in the new urban college suggested here, some conditions that already exist should clearly remain. It has been recognized for many years that it is very important for a planning student's learning experience to include workshops and internships. These experiences, however, need to be planned in the context of transdisciplinary teamwork integrated in both the convergent and divergent design premises.

Conclusion

The future of urban planning in the twenty-first century needs to have very different characteristics than it had in the twentieth century. In the twentieth century, urban planning training focused on urban design and transportation, with a great deal of attention given to citizen participation. These are all still necessary. Ultimately, however, an urban planner must be able to be a leader of interdisciplinary teams with broader geographic, environmental, economic, and social-psychological focus, especially given the growth of huge megacities—and especially with the continuing growth of artificial intelligence and other technological advances in energy, agriculture, transportation, and safe preservation of water resources.

In my view, urban planning needs to become a worldwide, leading professional concern—even more than law, medicine, education, and business.

References

Alonso, W. 1964. *Location and Land Use: Toward a General Theory of Land Rent.* Cambridge, MA: Harvard University Press.

Ayres, R. U., and E. H. Ayres. 2010. *Crossing the Energy Divide: Moving from Fossil Fuel Dependence to a Clean Energy Future.* Prentice-Hall.

Beatley, T. 2011. *Biophilic Cities: Integrating Nature into Urban Design and Planning.* Washington, DC: Island Press.

Bolan, R. S. 2017. *Urban Planning's Philosophical Entanglements: The Rugged, Dialectical Path from Knowledge to Action.* New York and London: Routledge Publishing.

Brown, T. 2009. *Change by Design: How Design Thinking Transforms Organizations and Inspires Innovation.* Pymble, Australia: HarperCollins e-books (http://www.harpercollinsebooks.com.au).

Bryson, J. R, L. Andres, and R. Mulhall, eds. 2018. *A Research Agenda for Regeneration Economies: Reading City-Regions.* Cheltenham, UK: Edward Elgar Publishing Limited.

Christaller, W. 1933. *Central Place Theory.* Jena, Germany: Gustav Fischer.

Daly, Herman. 1996. *Beyond Growth: The Economics of Sustainable Development.* Boston: Beacon Press.

Florida, Richard. 2017. *The New Urban Crisis: How Our Cities Are Increasing Inequality, Deepening Segregation, and Failing the Middle Class and What We Can Do About It.* New York: Basic Books

Gough, I. 2017. *Heat, Greed and Human Need: Climate Change, Capitalism and Sustainable Well-Being.* Cheltenham, UK: Edgar Elgar Publishing.

Hill, C. A., and R. W. Painter. 2015. *Better Bankers, Better Banks: Promoting Good Business through Contractual Appointments.* Chicago: University of Chicago Press.

Jackson, T. 2018. *Prosperity without Growth: Foundations for the Economy of Tomorrow.* 2nd ed. New York and London: Routledge.

Katz, B., and J. Nowak. 2017. *The New Localism: How Cities Can Thrive in the Age of Populism.* Washington, DC: Brookings Institute.

Lösch, A. 1940. *Die räumliche Or Emma's dnung der Wirtschaft.*

McCann, P. 2013. *Modern Urban and Regional Economics*. 2nd ed. Oxford, UK: Oxford University Press.

Moran, E. F. 2016. *Human Adaptability: An Introduction to Ecological Anthropology*. 3rd ed. Boulder, CO: Westview Press.

Moretti, E. 2013. *The New Geography of Jobs*. New York: Houghton Mifflin Harcourt Publishing Company.

Pfeiffer, D., and S. Cloutier. 2016. "Planning for Happy Neighborhoods." *Journal of the American Planning Association*: 267–79.

Rifkin, J. 2011. *The Third Industrial Revolution: How Lateral Power Is Transforming Energy, the Economy and the World*. New York: Macmillan.

Sachs, J. D. 2015. *The Age of Sustainable Development*. New York: Columbia University Press.

Sanchez, T. W., and N. Afzalan. 2014. "Mapping the Knowledge Domain of Planning." Paper presented at the Association of Collegiate Schools of Planning 54th Annual Conference. Philadelphia, PA.

Sassen, S. 2012. *Cities in a World Economy*. 4th ed. Los Angeles: Pine Forge Press.

Stein, S. (2019). *Capital City: Gentrification and the Real Estate State*. London, New York: Verso Books.

Stokols, D. 2018. *Social Ecology in the Digital Age: Solving Complex Problems in a Globalized World*. London, UK: Elsevier, Academic Press.

Wheeler, S. M., and T. Beatley, eds. 2004. *The Sustainable Urban Development Reader*. London and New York: Routledge.

Chapter 8

Epilogue

The irony is that America is filled with problem solvers, from governors and mayors to local businesses, philanthropies, civic action groups, and academia. The depth of talent in America's colleges and universities is remarkable, and not just in the famed schools that top the annual rankings. This means that every state, and virtually every metropolitan area, has top-flight expertise that can be called upon for local problem solving, or to put the pieces of a national program together from the bottom up. (Sachs 2017)

As Sir David Attenborough told the UN climate change conference in Poland (2018), "the collapse of our civilisations and the extinction of much of the natural world is on the horizon". We have even worked out, with scrupulous care, what we must do to avoid this or to mitigate the effects of climate change. We know what to do. We can see how to do it. There's only one problem: we do almost nothing.
(Editorial, Guardian: https://www.theguardian.com/commentisfree/2018/ dec/05/the-guardian-view-on-climate-change-too-much-too- soon?CMP=share_btn_fb&fbclid=IwAR3PPXNT6m-5oLJ- hF9C_Fhe8hhTrOCKQ j6nVpXuMkarT5GzBp5zAOUM8O0)

Early chapters have led to an extremely challenging picture of the future for us, our children, and our grandchildren. The main problem is the question of the planet Earth being a home for life of all descriptions—for human beings and many of the food species we rely on, along with other life species and vital environment and water resources. Protecting the ozone layer by diminishing CFC emissions was fundamental. Should the ozone layer significantly rise again, rays from the sun would raise the Earth's temperature to a point where no living creatures could survive. We also, however, need to be concerned about the impact of global warming on ocean levels, ocean temperatures, and ocean acidification. As pointed out in chapter 2, we need to be concerned about appropriate levels of nitrogen and phosphorus and other threats to environmental resources.

These are the fundamental questions as we see the rise of urban populations in the face of oligopolistic-corporatist economic dominance along with growing control of governments, the apparent decline of democracy, and the rise of new technologies, spawned in large measure by corporate entities. What will the global cities of the world be like in 2030 when the most powerful people—people in general command of economics, wealth, and government—tend to pay little attention to their impact on environmental threats? In addition, of course, there is good evidence that they are largely unconcerned about their power to generate unfair conditions of labor force and poverty.

This gives rise to the concerns expressed in the introduction: Garrett Hardin's *Tragedy of the Commons*, where today the commons is the *whole planet Earth*. I remember reading years ago Elinor Ostrom's challenge to Hardin's tragedy concept, where she had case studies of people solving the problem of appropriate treatment of the commons. One best example was a group of fishermen residing in a specific harbor, operating in an ocean environment where there was no private property. These entrepreneurs realized that unless they shared in goals, responsibilities, and accomplishments, they would soon be totally deprived of their fundamental food product—fish. Shared responsibility was required for not only maintaining the fish supply but also maintaining an occupation. It is clear today even the wealthiest leaders of oligopolies must be concerned about their local urban and planetary responsibilities. The ongoing Tragedy of the Commons should not be getting attention only from environmental scientists.

Moreover, will the current conditions as spelled out in the previous chapters allow us to meet the sustainable-development goals set forth by the United Nations? Can we end poverty in all its forms? To point out some of the key difficulties, the following summarily repeats the goals laid out in chapter 1 as reported by the UN for the year 2030:

People

We are determined to end poverty and hunger, in all their forms and dimensions, and to ensure that all human beings can fulfil their potential in dignity and equality and in a healthy environment.

Planet

We are determined to protect the planet from degradation, including through sustainable consumption and production, sustainably managing its natural resources and taking urgent action on climate change, so that it can support the needs of the present and future generations.

Prosperity

We are determined to ensure that all human beings can enjoy prosperous and fulfilling lives and that *economic, social and technological progress occurs in harmony with nature.* (Emphasis added.) (https://sustainabledevelopment.un.org/post2015/transforming our world)

Discussion thus far suggests that human use of the planet is moving 180 degrees in the opposite direction. There is one simple explanation as to why:

Money is still the main answer: Almost all prominent climate deniers are on the fossil-fuel take. However, ideology is also a factor: If you take environmental issues seriously, you are led to the need for government regulation of some kind, so rigid free-market ideologues don't want to believe that environmental concerns are real (although apparently forcing consumers to <u>subsidize coal</u> is fine). (Paul Krugman, "The Depravity of Climate-Change Denial," *New York Times*, November 26, 2018)

There is the growing formation of a broad array of sustainability-oriented civic organizations that can be found across the globe. Many are associations of local governments and global in membership, such as the Global Covenant of Mayors for Climate & Energy, C40 Cities, ICLEI 100 Resilient Cities,[57] Institute for Sustainable Communities, and International Institute for Sustainable Development. These are but a few of many such organizations that have periodic conferences with broad and often international participation.

Clearly, mayors and local governments have become appropriately and globally concerned with today's climate challenges. The urban areas of the world are dominant contributors to the destruction of environmental resources. Some mayors and city councils throughout the world have taken significant steps toward addressing some of these problems, as noted in chapter 6. An important law was passed by the state of California in the United States in September 2018. This law has a target of 100 percent carbon-free electricity by 2045, together with intermediate targets: 50 percent renewables by 2026; and 60 percent renewables by 2030. In the process of debate, petroleum and agricultural industries both provided opposition. Although the law does not have specific steps for achievement, there may well be legal suits in the processes of implementation. Other states are considering similar target programs as well; the state of Washington is another.   However, local governments make only a small dent in the powerful forces at work in planet Earth's Tragedy of the Commons. The overwhelming power of corporate, oligopolistic interests (and their power over national and regional governments) would appear be the true source of increasing global warming and demolition of environmental resources, together with issues of poverty, inequality, unemployment. The dominant role of fossil fuels (oil, natural gas, and coal) is still very strong. Solar and wind energy are still minorities in heating and electricity. Electric cars, trucks, and buses are still a very small minority in travel.

In the United States, with the help of newly elected members of Congress, climate change has now become an important political issue. With a change in the dominance of the corporate supporting party in the 2018 election, there is now a group in the House of Representatives strongly proposing a *Green New Deal*. A silent issue in the

---

[57] As noted in the last chapter, 100 Resilient Cities was funded by the Rockefeller Foundation. Unfortunately, in April 2019, the foundation shut it down.

US political world changed dramatically in the fourth quarter of the year 2018, so that newly elected people are strongly urging that attacking climate change is an important issue for the 2020 presidential election.[58]

New technologies may lead to creating new sustainability prospects, but they may also diminish labor force opportunity. Global corporatist behavior focuses on finding international locations where labor and resource costs are minimal (and taxes avoided). With existing trends, there is global evidence that only a small minority of human beings on the planet can fulfill their potential in wealth and affluent well-being. In the process of doing so, they are continually raising the menace of serious inequality everywhere in the world—including the better developed OECD countries in America, Europe, Japan, and so on. Finally, virtually all urban populations of today still move us in the wrong direction by relying heavily on automobile travel, truck commodity shipping, fossil fuel heating and air-conditioning, inadequate waste disposal, and many other forms of environmental damage.

It is abundantly clear that contemporary urban economic, social, and technological processes and behaviors *do not* occur in harmony with nature. What does this all mean as we face the UN forecasts of urban population? As the number of megacities rises, as the populations of moderate-sized cities also increase, as the populations living densely in coastal areas face increasing dangers from flooding and oceanic storms, what can be done in urban development to help move toward the UN's sustainable-development goals for 2030?

Considering the pervious chapters, one could have a pessimistic view of what life will be like for future generations. We can look at urbanization today, in the early twenty-first century, and sense that historically we have done a poor job of creating good urban living conditions, given the inequality, poverty, segregation, crime, and fundamental slum development, along with the dominance of the oligopolistic-corporatist economic system.

I am not suggesting pessimism. I think of the problems laid out here as significant challenges. Many disciplines are indeed working on these challenges. There is one near exception, however—the discipline of business —and this may be the most dominant challenge of the next twenty to thirty years: the global, oligopolistic-corporatist economy where greed coupled with power leads to achieving and continuing supremacy over governments, labor forces, and consumers. They are the dominant, self-serving, negative force in the planet Earth's Tragedy of the Commons.

---

[58] The United States Senate still has a strong Republican majority, so any effort to change corporate strength and influence may still involve a stalemate in trying to address the Tragedy of the Commons.

A New World of Economic Theory and Research

I am not an economist, although I have taken many courses in economics and have maintained interest in urban economics throughout my city planning career. However, the question of how we can prevent a full Tragedy of the Commons without in some way addressing a potential for true sustainable change in a dominant urban world controlled by the prevailing role of oligopolistic-corporatist economics is clearly of highest priority for all. Few economists appear to pay much attention to this problem. Growth economics still is widely supported in the profession. The support, as well, is largely focused on short-term forecasting, as many in the field are only concerned as to whether there can really be accurate quarterly (three-month) forecasts.

However, there is a small group of economists who refer to themselves as ecological economists, led over many years by Herman Daly. Today, leading scholars in this new field seek to establish fresh theoretical foundations for economic and environmental interrelated stability.

A recent book by England's prominent ecological economist Tim Jackson is one of the more up-to-date and interesting efforts that addresses what he calls "prosperity without growth." Jackson offers orientations that can help point to diminishing the power of corporatist, oligopolistic economics. In his foreword, he notes:

> Prosperity, in any meaningful sense of the term, is about the quality of our lives and relationships, about the resilience of our communities and about our sense of individual and collective meaning." (Jackson 2017, xxxviii)

His book provides probably the deepest discussion of what is involved in changing the current economy. First and foremost, he sees the economy as dominated by consumers. Fundamentally, the consumer economy does provide the foundations of human need: food, shelter, furniture, heat, electricity, and transportation. But he goes on to argue that the consumer-dominated market involves many additional *material* elements that are not fundamental to human need. Omitted from today's economic interests is the required need for physical, social and psychological health.

I was recently in the market for Bluetooth headphones so I could listen to music and news on my cell phone. I have searched out various options in sunglasses, neckties, and modern furniture. None of these in any way has anything to do with who I am or how I am related to my neighborhood, my employer, or my world. Material consumer pursuits are indicative of what Jackson refers to as a dominant but incorrect consumer economy. While I partially agree, my chapter 3 emphasizes the oligopolies currently dominating and includes strong corporations that today function somewhat independent of the consumer economy. These include the arms oligopoly and particularly the corporations engaged in finance, banking, venture capital, and asset management, along with the fossil fuel energy oligopoly. One might say that the pharmaceutical corporations discussed in chapter 3 are focused on health needs. However, their jacking up prices 300 to 600 percent in a short period of time suggests a propensity for taking a greedy advantage of health needs—not merely meeting such needs but robustly profiting from them.

Jackson's primary goal was probably best expressed as follows:

> It's good to have a clear philosophical vision. It's vital to have a sense of what we're aiming for, a direction for social progress. But we also need to articulate a path to take us there. And there's still a chance that the architecture of growth might play some role in that. Even though income is not the same as wellbeing, it is clearly in some sense functional in delivering at least some of the components of wellbeing. *Economic growth may not be a useful end in itself. It might still be the means to that end.*" (Ibid., 66) (Emphasis added.)

Jackson then goes on to emphasize:

> The task of the economy is to deliver and to enable prosperity. But prosperity is not synonymous with material wealth and its requirements go beyond material sustenance. Rather, prosperity has to do with our ability to flourish: physically, psychologically and socially. Beyond sheer subsistence or survival, prosperity hangs on our ability to participate meaningfully in the life of society. This task is as much social and psychological as it is material. (Ibid., 121)

One of the major points in Jackson's final chapter is the relationship of the economy and government. His emphasis is that government needs to be more firmly in control of economic activity, particularly with respect to meeting fundamental human needs. Jackson is a resident of England, and while it may be possible for stronger government control in the UK and perhaps also in Europe (and clearly in China), it would seem not to be the case in the United States—the leader in the global, oligopolistic-corporatist economy. Corporate control and domination of US government seems almost overwhelming. Corporations have been strongly supported by the US Supreme Court, and they have the monetary superiority to control legislative lobbying and election-campaign funding. The result of the 2018 election saw some rejection of Republican control of all branches of government. Today, the House of Representatives is dominated by the Democratic Party, yet the Senate, the White House, and the Supreme Court are still Republican and thus corporatist dominated.

They also similarly dominate some state and local government policy and practice (chapter 4). They clearly overshadow individual voters.

What is most important in Jackson's book is the philosophical foundation as to how we conceive of a human economy. Monetary profit as the one and only motivation for economic theory is limited and wholly insufficient in pursuit of foundational human welfare. With small business, profits perhaps are singularly justified, as Adam Smith argued. However, Jackson points out that even Adam Smith was disturbed by a monopolistic economy, and Smith argued that governments should exercise control. The underlying pushes to monopoly yielding an oligopolistic economy severely detracts from the fundamental goals of human well-being. Benjamin Barber's suggestion that mayors of cities should rule and that national governments are largely dysfunctional is intriguing. The relationship of power between different levels of rule is clearly in question here.

However, I would argue that pursuing sustainable goals may indeed involve deep inquiry into theoretical and practical institutional design (Bolan 1991). Our nations (our citizens, our voters) are truly the captives of our economy. Mayors can accomplish some things as needed but not everything that is needed. Today we have global norms, customs, and laws that vary somewhat between countries, but economic enterprise is by far the strongest institution.

A recent author, Pulitzer Prize–winner Steven Pearlstein, has given close attention to reforms he sees as necessary in the United States. He sums them up in his last chapter:

> A constitutional amendment putting limits on special interest money. A guaranteed minimum income in exchange for national service. Profit sharing for all employees. Ending class segregation in public schools. Restoring competition to overly consolidated markets through more aggressive antitrust enforcement, reform of copyright and patent law and greater reliance on customer-owned financial institutions. Requiring public companies to be transparent about their purposes and priorities. That these sound like radical and politically unachievable ideas speaks to the paucity of our political imagination and the lack of faith in our institutions to adapt to new circumstances. (Pearlstein 2018, 203).

Pearlstein's proposals are excellent, and I have only one serious criticism: there is no real attention in his book to the global character of the oligopolistic- corporatist economy—the movement of corporate headquarters to tax-free countries, to countries where mergers and acquisitions are easier to achieve (such as the US firm Monsanto and the German firm Bayer), and countries where labor costs are a small fraction of what would need to be paid to US workers.

Another recent publication is also concerned with corporate dominance in the United States. Columbia law professor Tim Wu has published a first-rate book seeking to return to an antitrust legal environment in the United States. His book is a history of antitrust legislation giving attention to the many corporate monopolies that emerged in the early twentieth century. At the outset, he restored the thinking of Brandeis:

> If [Brandeis] had a unifying principle, politically and economically, it is what we have said: that concentrated power in any form is dangerous, that institutions should be built to human scale, and society should pursue human ends. Every institution, public and private, runs the risks of taking on a life of its own, putting its own interests above those of the humans it was supposedly created to serve. (Wu 2018, 43)

Wu argues that too much concentrated economic power translates into too much political power, and we see that today. We need a strong check on private power, and Wu argues the more concentrated the industry, the more corrupted we can expect the political process to be.

> Some effort to revive the antitrust laws may be an inevitability in a nation founded on principles of anti-monopoly, equality, and decentralized power. What should be done? It's not enough to demand change without providing an agenda that enjoys legal legitimacy, can make use of the best economic tools, and is usable by enforcers, judges, and industry itself. (Wu 2018, 127)

Finally, there are ideas that urban planners should give to local urban economic development. One possibility is the potential design of networks by which business enterprises on a metropolitan scale could create energy links to significantly reduce waste pollution. One of the earliest examples of this was a program set up in the 1980s in Kalundborg, Denmark. It was described in a recent book by Paul Hawkin:

> In Kalundborg, a coal-fired power plant, an oil refinery, a pharmaceutical company specializing in biotechnology, a Sheetrock plant, concrete producers, a producer of sulfuric acid, the municipal heating authority, a fish farm, some greenhouses, local farms, and other enterprises work cooperatively together. (Hawkin 2010, 73)

This provides a good historical example of linking energy use, and this has been a feature of many existing cities.[59] The negative aspect of the Denmark example is that the network got its start from a coal-fired power plant, so that while energy waste was continually reused by the participants, the ultimate waste was still negative.

A recent book by Jeremy Rifkin suggests that with today's advancements in artificial intelligence, along with solar, wind, and hydro energy, every building in an urban area can be both a consumer and producer of

---

[59] When I worked in Boston in the 1960s, many downtown buildings were linked together for energy use.

energy, so that all occupied and used buildings (commercial and residential) are part of an energy network linked by social communication technology that overall minimizes waste. Additionally, the waste produced is environmentally positive. Rifkin puts this in his overall title of *The Third Industrial Revolution*. Rifkin has been working closely with cities in Europe. He sees the convergence of new communication technologies with new energy systems as fundamental to a totally new form of global life and suggests that it may also untangle today's oligopolistic, corporatist economy.

From the perspective of urban economic-development planning, this does offer an interesting new perspective on future land-use planning.

The Whole World Needs to Pay More Attention to the Tragedy of the Commons

The Tragedy of the Commons has its most significant causes from the world's urban communities. Thus, city foresight today is critical for the survival of future generations. Foresight is also highly necessary for determining human needs in the coming years, beyond the psychological motives of greed and power that reflect the dominance of the corporate economy.

Urban planning does not attract a great deal of attention in broad public discourse. It does get some attention at a local level where urban planning primarily is deemed to be of only local concern. Most discussion focuses on zoning changes, developer-proposed buildings, traffic, parking, neighborhood plans, parks, and so on. These discussions are located primarily in the local newspaper (*not* local TV or radio). With the growth of the global urban population and with the current significant social and economic problems (inequality, poverty, joblessness, poor housing conditions, racial segregation, crime), there needs to be much broader attention not only to the growing urban population but also to the growing oligopolistic-corporatist economy, the weakening of governments and democracy, and the rise of technological change drastically influencing labor force opportunity and social life. Urban problems are no longer strictly local; they have regional, international, and global impacts.

Research and study of world problems is happening in many academic disciplines, although the scholars focus on specific problems within their distinctive discipline, while not necessarily seeing those problems as significantly related to other problems, or other disciplines, or as uniquely urban. If urban population increases by 2.5 billion by 2050, attention needs to be paid to the interdisciplinary challenges and opportunities that result. I would argue that we need to pay much closer attention to issues of *institutional design*. The oligopolistic-corporatist world truly dominates the planet Earth, and the key question is how that can be changed.

We tend to think of institutions as permanent social norms of some kind or another. I noted in a recent publication that John Searle, a social philosopher at the University of California, Berkeley, identified what he calls "deep-seated structural institutions": money, private property, marriage, government (Searle 2010, 91).

> When I was very young, I saw all these as definitely constant unchanging laws customs and practices—that is until my parents decided to divorce. In today's terms private property has some deep changes going on—particularly with the rise of condominium and cooperative residences and a seriously declining market in shopping malls. Money is becoming an increasingly digitized custom—pieces of paper and round metal coins are being used less and less. In the United States, the current divorce rate ranges from 41% to 50%, so marriage as a deep-seated structural institution is actually undergoing meaningful change (including the new legality of same-sex marriage). (Bolan 2018, xxii–xxiii.)

The question is, how can we approach the current corporate, formal world dominance and create an institutional world of sustainability—environmental, political, economic, urban, and social?

In previous research, I saw the process of institutional change as part of the dialectical interaction of normative structure and collective agency. Included in normative structure are rules for changing rules, and we obviously need to pay close attention to these. But the critical dimension of institutional change lies in both individual and collective action. This is important, as has been seen in the recent legal provisions of same-sex marriage and use of marijuana, along with the rise of the #Me-Too Movement.

A recent event provides a good illustration of potential for corporate institutional change. Thousands of Google employees around the world took a day off the job to protest allegations of sexual misconduct against top executives, after the allegations were publicized by the *New York Times*. Those taking the day off also were seeking more aggressive steps for gender pay and equity and inclusive hiring practices (*Minneapolis Star-Tribune*, November 2, 2018, pages D1 and D6).

This is an illustration of a useful conceptualization of the institutional change process set forth some years ago by John M. Bryson and Barbara Crosby (1993). They suggested the framework for institutional change included forums, arenas, and courts. Forums are frameworks for communication and discussion and involve the beginning steps for institutional design and change. This may start with the kind of action taken at the Google corporation's worldwide locations. They also start with the global entities noted above. From this, more organized forum discussions can take place, leading to formal arenas for decision-making.

Hopefully the Google employees have initiated steps toward arenas for changing corporate behavior.[60] Hopefully the people active in the Global Covenant of Mayors for Climate & Energy, C40 Cities, ICLEI 100 Resilient Cities, Institute for Sustainable Communities, and International Institute for Sustainable Development realize they need to create forums for change.

Corporate leaders need to become more involved in adopting social responsibility, especially those leading in oligopolies. They need to interlock in new discussion forums, *not* to increase greed and control (and especially not to involve bribery, tax evasion, money hiding, or other too common illegal activity) but rather to be jointly immersed in planning an urban economic world that undertakes managing environmental and human sustainability beyond corporate growth, executive wealth, and severe inequality. Corporate leaders must see themselves as comparable to the fishermen in Ostrom's analysis of commons responsibility. They not only need to work to save the planet but also to continue to have a planet with worthwhile jobs.

Some evidence of this can be found in a new online forum for corporate ethical responsibility. It is an organization called Ethical Corporation, and its mission is to help businesses around the globe do the right thing by their customers and the world. They believe[61] this is how to ensure a future for all while making

---

[60] Courts are a general term used by Bryson and Crosby where formal structures are created for carrying out and managing decisions.

[61] Another similar group is an organization called Corporate Accountability. This groups exhibit a bit more hostility to corporations, but their role is to hold the corporate world accountable.

good business sense. They provide topical and insightful business intelligence and meeting places. The organization puts it this way:

> We provide business intelligence to more than 3,000 multinational companies every year. Our customers are also NGOs, think-tanks, academia, governments and consultancies. We publish the leading responsible business magazine, website, and research reports. Our conferences are widely recognized as the best in the field.

Corporate leaders should fundamentally be equally concerned with basic *sustainable* human needs beyond the fashion interests of consumer-market buyers. This also means stopping the historical patterns of exploiting and quashing labor forces. This as well includes focusing on limiting inequality and balancing consumer expenditure and fundamental needs. In short, the corporate world needs to reestablish its overall social responsibility—not merely obligations to shareholders, board members, and individual executives. Every corporation, and every corporate leader, has fundamental responsibility to *all people* that includes not only health and well-being but fundamentally staying within the planetary resource limits that affect everyone.

Corporations need to stop degrading their workers; they are human beings not only working but also living in human families and communities. Employees are not mere corporate production tools. Corporations also need to stop controlling their consumers. The pharmaceutical oligopoly is perhaps the worst in this regard. Today, the sicker you are, the more the pharmaceutical corporations can exploit you.

Another group that needs to become involved in a comprehensive forum for urban sustainability is philanthropic leaders. The Ford Foundation and the Rockefeller Foundation are two that are doing work focused on urban resilience and sustainability. Generally, philanthropic organizations tend to focus on very specific, specialized areas. The Gates Foundation, for example, focuses on worldwide health problems in addition to agricultural issues. Strong areas of philanthropic concern are promoting democratic governance, education, human rights, social justice, and help for immigration populations. Some philanthropies focus on childhood development, arts programs, and helping other local philanthropies.[62] Today, however, given the

---

[62] Source: https://www.devex.com/news/top-10-philanthropic-foundations-a-primer-75508.

expected concentration of people in urban areas, philanthropies need to give increasing attention to urbanity problems. As argued by Sally Uren in the most recent magazine of the *Ethical Corporation*:

> Many millions of philanthropic capital are deployed to deal with the symptoms, not the cause of catastrophic environmental and social disasters. (Sally Uren, *Ethical Corporation*, January 2019, p. 10)

The field of journalism also needs to focus more attention on urban problems and become a more active member in the forum for sustainability. Three events of 2018, however, have led to increased journalistic coverage: (1) the United Nations IPCC report of the need to aim at the limit of 1.5° Centigrade, (2) the congressionally ordered updated report of US governmental environmental scientists, and (3) the international environmental conference in Poland aimed at upgrading the Paris Agreement of 2015.[63]

In October 2018, the UNIPCC issued a report signifying that rather than aiming to limit climate warming to 2° Centigrade, we should really be aiming at a target limited to 1.5° Centigrade. The planetary global temperature has been moving faster than previously recorded. The dangers of global warming were seen in their report to be more rapidly becoming more serious and needing more immediate activity. The US report in November 2018 and the International Conference in Katowice, Poland, in December created significant increases in media attention, and this has continued so that, at the time of this writing, there is daily attention given to climate warming and environmental destruction.

These events have dramatically enhanced public attention to climate change and environmental destruction. This has included the significant upsurge of environmental concerns in the political arena with the rise of the Green New Deal. Journalists now pay attention almost daily to climate change issues, whereas prior to October 2018, one hardly ever saw any attention.

Journalism, in all its technological capability, is a key instrument in creating broad general understanding of the problems and opportunities of the growing urban population. There have been some key books written

---

[63] The Polish conference, however, has surfaced countries aiming at using fossil fuel resources for an indefinite future. These include the United States, Saudi Arabia, Russia, and Kuwait (*Minneapolis Star Tribune*, Dec. 11, 2018, p. A3).

by journalists that have provided significant reporting on contemporary conditions, many of which have been influential in my writing (including Mayer 2016; Lynn 2010; Kuttner 2018).

Journalism needs to give constant and ostentatious attention to the Tragedy of the Commons. There should be more media reports on scientific publications and conferences, more attention to urban area efforts. The forecasts of urban and climate change dangers are concerned with disastrous effects in the next twelve to thirty years. An auto manufacturer announced in mid-2018 that they were going to slow down the manufacture of small cars to meet their increasing demands for SUV vehicles—cars with significantly higher levels of CO_2 emissions. It appeared in the media for a single day, with no one expressing an opinion as to whether this was a wise decision regarding pollution or global warming (it was obviously a decision to increase SUV car sales and profits).[64] The annual car report in the magazine *Consumer Reports* shows that brand-new SUVs range between twenty-two and twenty-eight miles per gallon—much worse than small cars or hybrids (*Consumer Reports*, April 2019)

Universities need to become stronger leaders in the forum on sustainability. There is increasing need to include global university presidents, board members, and other scholarly leaders. Michael Crow, president of Arizona State University, stated the educational challenge very well:

> Academic culture has not evolved sufficiently in its ability to mount adequate responses at scale and in real time to the progressively accelerating complexity that marks contemporary life. This lack of adaptive capacity is nowhere more evident than in the institutional posture of our universities to address grand challenges— one need only think of global climate change, air and water pollution, overpopulation, hunger, poverty, extinction of species, exhaustion of natural resources, and destruction of ecosystems. (Quoted in Stokols 2018, 319; originally in *BioScience* 60, no. 7 [2010]: 488–89.)

---

[64] More recently, General Motors indicated that they too were giving up small cars in favor of SUVs and were closing three US factories and two Canadian factories, with job losses close to fourteen thousand.

Universities have significant responsibilities in the contemporary world. We live in a world where there is strong devotion by many to laissez-faire theory of economics. Yet the world of the twenty-first century indicates that theory is no longer appropriate or in any way correct. As pointed out at the beginning of this chapter, new economic theory needs to be formulated and tested with significant dimensions of social responsibility. This is especially true for business schools. As reported in previous chapters, the high level of dubious and even illegal activity among today's corporate leaders suggests that their business school training did not offer a strong orientation toward social responsibility. Business schools should be providing emphasis on treating laborers as human beings rather than simple instruments of production.[65] They should push their students, after graduation, to work internships in communities, helping in the alleviation of poverty and reducing inequality to more humanistic levels. They should give greater attention to the reduction of pollution and to alleviating climate change. They should be training people to be responsible to more than just shareholders and investors. Business schools should also include curriculum and research in global economic sustainability.[66]

Medical and public health schools already give close attention to urban health and mental health and the fundamental, underlying social causes of malady. Law schools also tend to focus on urban problems since urban areas tend to be the strongest in crime—both physical crime and social crime (investment fraud, bribery, money laundering, tax evasion, etc.). As expected, they refer to their problems as legal problems, not urban problems, even though they predominantly occur in urban areas. Urban areas are most susceptible to crime, not only violent crime in the streets but also business crime in the highest corporate offices.

Schools of education should focus beyond classroom education, addressing poverty and racial and religious diversity, particularly in the growing urban settings. In the United States, school management increasingly needs to pay attention to everything from an adequate budget in a technologically changing

---

[65] The ways business leaders treat their workers was well described by Robert Kuttner in his book *Can Democracy Survive Local Capitalism?* (chapter 5, 2018). They not only have managed to suppress union membership and power, but there is also an expansion of temporary or part-time employment lacking any health, retirement, or other benefits.

[66] I did a survey of the websites of the top ten business schools in the United States. The top three showed no sign of *any* ethics course in their curricula. Of the top ten, only half had a course that was called Business Ethics.

world to protection from mass school shooting (that would also include the role of education in health and mental health).

Universities should also pay much more attention to urban planning. The study of urban planning should not be by only small groups of faculty and students, barely visible within architecture schools or schools of public administration. As promoted in chapter 7, urban planning should be an equal university enterprise along with law, medicine, education, and business. It should focus on *interdisciplinary learning and application*. Urban problems of today and the future extend far beyond architecture, engineering, and land-use zoning. Climate problems, created historically and increasingly by growing urbanization since the nineteenth century, now need top-priority academic focus.

Universities are beginning to pay more attention to the problems of sustainability. A few United States universities have begun to create training programs in sustainability. Notable among these is Arizona State University with its School of Sustainability (that includes its accredited program in urban planning). Internationally, the University of Cambridge in the United Kingdom is another, as is the Lahti University in Finland. The University of British Columbia and the University of Toronto are Canadian universities offering programs in sustainability. There are also signs of interuniversity research with government help, as exemplified in a new joint program with Duke University and the University of Minnesota, who will eventually create a multi-university network in sustainability science.

Finally, there should be greater focus on encouraging young people to become involved in the future problems I have identified here. Journalism, philanthropy, and educational institutions should do a great deal more in terms of significantly increasing the number of people professionally prepared to deal with the growing urban and climate problems.

Recruiting, in my mind, really should start in high school with the study of civics giving greater attention to the problems of global urbanity and sustainability. There are clearly high school students today who are aware of this. On March 15, 2019, high school students from many countries around the world (given the power of social communication) held their Youth Climate Strike, arguing that parents and other adults should be acting on climate change today.

Conclusion

Given the forecasts presented in all the previous chapters, the future from now to 2030 and 2050 promises to be extremely challenging. The history of urbanization since the industrial age has created a fundamental array of environmental, economic, governmental, and social challenges. If we ignore these challenges, the future of the lives of human beings and other animals and flora and fauna in the planet's resources could be eliminated. Indeed, increasing urbanization needs to be addressed while we are immersed in a world of uncertainty.

We need to give stronger attention to deeper institutional, economic, social, political, and technical change so that we can carry out what we need to do to overcome the Tragedy of the Commons.

Finally, as noted above, there should be greater focus on globally encouraging young people to become involved in urban and environmental challenges. Recruiting should start in high school with the study of civics, giving greater fundamental attention to the problems and opportunities of global urbanity.

This recruiting challenge is one derived from deeper and more complex challenges that I have outlined in the various chapters of this book. Chapter 2 laid out projections of the United Nations Population Division. There are strong trend lines indicating major growth in urban populations by 2030 (now slightly more than a decade away) and 2050, the midpoint of the twenty-first century. Chapter 2 also raised the planetary issues that such urbanization would likely cause.

In chapter 3, I explored what I consider one of the most dangerous problems facing the global future—the rise of domination by an all-powerful, global, oligopolistic-corporatist economy. Chapter 4, of course, laid out the existing background whereby the dominant corporatist economy strongly controls the institutions of governance, not only in the northern developed world but also in the Southern nations of the globe. This dominance, I suggest, is pushing the decline of democracy globally, including the so-called American democracy.

This corporatist dominance is also aided by the technological innovations outlined in chapter 5. These are artificial intelligence innovations we are now experiencing and what we will be likely experiencing over the next fifteen to twenty-five years. In the year 2000, today's broad expanse of communications technology was just really beginning. Only a few years later, a major corporatist oligopoly came into being with the dominance of Google, Facebook, Amazon, Comcast, Time Warner, Verizon, AT&T, Apple, and subsidiary corporate partners. This rapid arrival of a new oligopoly has had significant impacts on the world labor force. It also has significant impacts in enabling the financing of mergers and acquisitions that support and strengthen corporatist oligopolies at very little cost, using already developed artificial intelligence.

Finally, in chapter 6, I raised the issue of land use. Clearly housing is a most critical issue facing all countries on the planet. But urban land use is not strictly an urban only question. In the first instance, much land focused on food production has meant a significant depletion of water and woodland resources. This in turn raises global emissions that severely challenge the environmental health of the planet. In addition, the nature of urban development experienced in the last half of the twentieth century, particularly in the United States, involved significant urban sprawl that is a distinct problem for urban planning. Finally, of course, is the role of corporate oligopolies in building urban expansion and extracting the earth's land resources involving coal, petroleum, uranium, and other underground metallic and chemical resources.

The important point is to take these challenges outlined in the previous chapters seriously but not too literally. The future is still impossible to predict precisely. The challenge of global warming does seem inevitable, yet there are many variations in the way that a specific urban area may be facing it. There may also be growing resistance to the global oligopolistic-corporatist economy in the growing global inequality. Of course, untreated adverse global physical and mental health could be a strong factor in limiting urban population growth.

With global warming, urban planning has taken on a new and encouraging focus, the concept of *resiliency*. Resiliency implies the ability to absorb the effects of a completely unpredictable and devastating event while being able to survive and restore the viability of the victimized communities. The increasing frequency of disastrous events around the globe in recent years has seen urban officials increasingly involved in planning for emergency preparedness. These events (hurricanes, tornadoes, forest fires, and flooding) stimulate debate about their cause, as to whether it stems from global phenomena or local circumstances. Whatever the cause, urban officials realize such events pose a significant challenge.

Perhaps I have begun only to scratch the surface of what is happening in the world economically, politically, and socially. Today we also are experiencing worldwide immigration problems. The most prominent example is the situation in Syria, where people have been seeking access to Europe to escape from devastating war led by a murderous dictator and to find a safe and happy home environment. European countries now have factions vigorously resisting immigration. Eastern European countries, having escaped from the Soviet Union in the 1990s, are trying to build walls and retreat from efforts to create a democracy.

While it is not clear whether a new physical wall will be built on the US-Mexican border, those currently in political power are erecting a metaphorical, virtual wall. This is a problem that none of my earlier chapters really tackled. Nonetheless, it is a significant addition to the need for understanding the UN's sustainable-development goals—basic human needs.

For young people choosing a future in the urban planning profession, all the above issues are paramount, even at the local level, where most urban planners are traditionally hired. Should the future trends and challenges I have cited be realized, the planner's task is to align people as broadly as possible around common inclusive goals. When conflict exists, the planner's task is to turn it into a creative opportunity rather than a destructive one.

There is little doubt in my mind that the future education of urban planners needs to be broader than simply four semesters over two years (as discussed in chapter 7). The programs of other professions (such as law, medicine, education, and business) long ago understood their educational requirements arising from expanding knowledge bases and greater problem complexity. This entails much broader creative concerns over the design process, beyond physical artifacts working toward improving social relations (Pfeiffer and Cloutier 2016).

This finally reminds me of a telephone conversation with the leading urban planner John Friedmann (who sadly recently passed away), in which he noted, "What might an urban planner become as we face the future?" (personal conversation in 2016).

References

Alonso, W. 1964. *Location and Land Use: Toward a General Theory of Land Rent.* Cambridge, MA: Harvard University Press.

Ayres, R. U., and E. H. Ayres. 2010. *Crossing the Energy Divide Moving from Fossil Fuel Dependence to a Clean-Energy Future.* Prentice Hall.

Barber, B. 2014. *If Mayors Ruled the World: Dysfunctional Nations, Rising Cities.* Paperback edition. New Haven: Yale University Press.

Beatley, T. 2011. *Biophilic Cities: Integrating Nature into Urban Design and Planning.* Washington, DC: The Island Press.

Bolan, R. S. 2017. *Urban Planning's Philosophical Entanglements: The Rugged, Dialectical Path from Knowledge to Action.* New York and London: Routledge Publishing.

Bolan, R. S. 1991. "Planning and Institutional Design." *Planning Theory* 5, no. 6: 7–34.

Bolan, R. S. 1994. "Planning and the Dialectics of Institutional Design." Paper for the 36th Annual Conference of the Association of Collegiate Schools of Planning, Phoenix, Arizona.

Brown, T. 2009. *Change by Design: How Design Thinking Transforms Organizations and Inspires Innovation.* Pymble, Australia: HarperCollins e-books (http://www.harpercollinsebooks.com.au).

Bryson, J., and B. Crosby. 2005. *Leadership for the Common Good.* 2nd ed. San Francisco: Jossey-Bass.

Castells, M. 2010. *The Rise of the Network Society,* second edition. Malden, MA: Wiley-Blackwell.

Christaller, W. 1933. *Central Place Theory.* Jena, Germany: Gustav Fischer.

Daly, Herman. 1996. *Beyond Growth: The Economics of Sustainable Development.* Boston: Beacon Press.

Florida, Richard. 2017. *The New Urban Crisis: How Our Cities Are Increasing Inequality, Deepening Segregation, and Failing the Middle Class and What We Can Do About It.* New York: Basic Books.

Gough, I. 2017. *Heat, Greed and Human Need: Climate Change, Capitalism and Sustainable Well-Being.* Cheltenham, UK: Edgar Elgar Publishing.

Hawken, Paul. 2010. *The Ecology of Commerce: The Revised Edition.* New York: Harper Collins.

Hill, C. A., and R. W. Painter. 2015. *Better Bankers, Better Banks: Promoting Good Business through Contractual Appointments.* Chicago: University of Chicago Press.

Jackson, T. 2017. *Prosperity without Growth: Foundations for the Economy of Tomorrow.* 2nd ed. London and New York: Routledge.

Katz, B., and J. Nowak. 2017. *The New Localism: How Cities Can Thrive in the Age of Populism.* Washington, DC: Brookings Institute.

Krasney, M. E., and K. G. Tidball. 2015. *Civic Ecology: Adaptation and Transformation from the Ground up.* Cambridge, MA: MIT Press.

Kuttner, R. 2018. *Can Democracy Survive Global Capitalism?* New York: WW Norton and Company.

Lösch, A. 1940. *Die räumliche Or Emma's dnung der Wirtschaft.*

McCann, P. 2013. *Modern Urban and Regional Economics.* 2nd ed. Oxford, UK: Oxford University Press.

Moran, E. F. 2016. *Human Adaptability: An Introduction to Ecological Anthropology.* 3rd ed. Boulder, CO: Westview Press.

Moretti, E. 2013. *The New Geography of Jobs.* New York: Houghton Mifflin Harcourt Publishing Company.

Pearlstein, Steven. 2018. *Can American Capitalism Survive? Why Greed Is Not Good, Opportunity Is Not Equal, And Fairness Won't Make Us Poor.* New York: Saint Martin's Press.

Pfeiffer, D., and S. Cloutier. 2016. "Planning for Happy Neighborhoods." *Journal of the American Planning Association*: 267–79.

Rifkin, J. 2011. *The Third Industrial Revolution: How Lateral Power Is Transforming Energy, the Economy and the World.* New York: Macmillan.

Sachs, J. D. 2015. *The Age of Sustainable Development.* New York: Columbia University Press.

Sachs, J. D. 2017. *Building the New American Economy: Smart, Fair, and Sustainable.* New York: Columbia University Press.

Sanchez, T. W., and N. Afzalan. 2014. "Mapping the Knowledge Domain of Planning." Paper presented at the Association of Collegiate Schools of Planning 54th Annual Conference. Philadelphia, PA.

Sassen, S. 2012. *Cities in a World Economy.* 4th ed. Los Angeles: Pine Forge Press.

Stokols, D. 2018. *Social Ecology in the Digital Age: Solving Complex Problems in a Globalized World*. London, UK: Elsevier Academic Press.

Stokols, D., et al. 2003. "Increasing the Health Promotive Capacity of Human Environments." *American Journal of Health Promotion* 18, no. 1: 4–13.

United Nations Intergovernmental Panel on Climate Change (IPCC), 2018. *Global Warming of 1.5 Degrees.* http://www.ipcc.ch/report/sr15/.

Wheeler, S. M., and T. Beatley, eds. 2004. *The Sustainable Urban Development Reader.* London and New York: Routledge.

Wu, T. 2018. *The Curse of Bigness: Antitrust in the New Gilded Age.* New York: Columbia Global Reports.

Index

Foreign Corrupt Practices Act (FCPA) (1977), 66–69, 68*f*, 69*t*, 173

foreign land acquisition, 148

foreign tax haven countries, 90–91

forest fires, impact of on urban population growth, 26, 27

Fort Trumbull (New London, Connecticut), corporatism in, 169–170

Fortune 500 corporations, geographic spread of, 38, 39*f*

fossil fuels, use of, 49, 185, 186, 188, 196n63

Foxconn, 170

fracking, 110

Framework Convention on Climate Change (UNFCCC), 7

free market economy, 6, 8, 42, 43, 45, 77, 184

Freedom Works, 86

freshwater use, in Neo-Malthusian theory, 32*f*

Friedmann, John, 202

Frigidaire, 90

Fruit of the Loom, 60

future, forecasting of, 26

G

Garden Cities New Towns program, 130

Gates, Bill, 95

Gates Foundation, 195

Gateway, 38

GEICO, 60

General Dynamics, 58

General Electric, 87

General Motors, 48*t*, 52, 53, 65, 90, 197n64

genetically designed food, as agricultural technology, 116

Gilens, Martin, 81

Global 2000, 7

global corporatism, history of, 39–41

Global Covenant of Mayors for Climate & Energy, 152, 185, 194

global financial regulation, removal of, 41

global wages, differential in, 66

global warming
　challenges of, 201
　as contributor to Tragedy of Commons, 6
　dangers of, 7, 50, 196
　doing more to limit, 31
　effect of urban development on, 17, 166
　and history of urban living since Industrial Revolution, 3
　impact of cost of petroleum on, 109
　impact of natural gas on, 110
　impact of transportation of construction materials on, 34
　increased awareness of, 1
　local governmental concern about, 152
　true source of increasing of, 185
　wealthier human beings' contributions to, 165

Goldman Sachs, 62n19

Good Humor Ice Cream Bar, 90

Google, 53, 54, 84, 100, 102, 125, 146, 193–194

Gough, Ian, 95, 165

governance/government
　capitalism as not able to exist without, 78
　corporate control of, 76–79
　incentives from for economic development, 148–150

government regulation
　minimization of/limiting of/relaxation of, 7, 8, 10, 36, 63, 77
　need for, 184
　removal of global financial regulation, 41

government shutdowns, 79n25

Great Britain, Garden Cities New Towns program, 130

infrastructural viability sensors, as agricultural technology, 116

Institute for Sustainable Communities, 152, 185, 194

Institution on Taxation and Economic Policy (ITEP), 87, 88, 89, 91

institutional change, 193–194

institutional design, needing to pay closer attention to, 193

Intel, 53

Intergovernmental Panel on Climate Change (IPCC) (UN), 7, 196

International Council for Local Environmental Initiatives (ICLEI), 152, 185, 194

International Institute for Sustainable Development, 152, 185, 194

International Monetary Fund, 41

Investopedia, 64–65

invisible hand, 42

Ireland, relocation of US corporations to, 89–90

"Is Capitalism Compatible with Democracy?" (Merkel), 93–94

Isard, Walter, 170

ITEP (Institution on Taxation and Economic Policy), 87, 88, 89, 91

J

Jackson, Tim, 49, 77, 171, 187, 188–189

Jawaharlal Nehru National Urban Renewal Mission, 140

JBS-Friboi, purchase of Swift & Company by, 38

JC Penney, 111

Jefferson, Thomas, 76

Jensen, Nathan M., 149

Johnson, Simon, 65

Johnson & Johnson, 84

The John M. Olin Foundation, 86

journalism, role of in focusing more attention on urban problems and sustainability, 196–197, 199

J.P. Morgan Chase, 62, 88

just-in-time inventory system, impact of, 52

K

K Street firms, 82

Kalundborg, Denmark, as example of linking energy use, 191

Kansas City, Missouri, incentives for economic development in, 149

Katowice Conference (2018), 1, 7, 71, 196

Katz, B., 105

Kavanaugh, Brett, 82

Kelo, Susette, 169

Kelo v. City of New London, 169

Kennedy, Anthony, 82

Kenya, housing in, 144

Keynesian theory, 41

Klondike, 90

Koch brothers, 86

Koch Foods, 59

Kraft, B. R., 106

Kraft Foods, 60

Krugman, Paul, 170

Kuttner, Robert, 41, 90, 91

Kyoto Protocol (1997), 7

L

labor costs, 41, 66, 89, 147, 148, 160, 190

labor force, impact of technological innovation on, 118–124, 119*f*

labor unions, 70, 71, 81, 86–87, 95, 103, 173, 198n65

Lahti University (Finland), training program in sustainability, 199

laissez-faire, 41, 42, 198

petroleum, use of, 11, 40, 45, 49–50, 92, 108–109, 185, 201. *See also* oil, use of

Pew Charitable Trust, 135

Pfizer, 84, 169

pharmaceutical field, microeconomics in, 44–45

pharmaceutical oligopoly, 55–57, 57*t*

Pharmaceutical Research and Manufactures of America (PhRMA), 84

philanthropy, role of in forum for urban sustainability, 195–196, 199

phosphorus cycle, in Neo-Malthusian theory, 32*f*

Pilgrims Pride, 59

Pinochet, Augusto, 93

Pittsburgh, Pennsylvania, as modern center of robotic invention and engineering, 105, 171

Planning Accreditation Board, 158, 159–160*b*

planning theory, 158n49

Platform, 54

Plumer, Brad, 113

pollution, 2n1, 3, 6, 7n3, 17, 42, 42n13, 50, 109, 110, 112, 191, 197, 198

Popper, Karl, 26

Popular Mechanics, on new technology, 100

population growth
    as contributor to Tragedy of Commons, 3
    forecast on, 10, 127
    in urban areas, 16–34, 18*f*
    in urban coastal regions, 28, 30*t*

Porter, Michael, 170

poultry, production of, 59–60

Pradhan Mantri Awas Yojana (PMAY), 140

precision agriculture, 116

prefabricated housing, use of, 145

privacy
    broad-scale invasion of, 102, 117
    technology for enhancement of, 101

professional education, in American universities, 157, 158

"prosperity without growth," 187

public housing, 12, 175, 176

public-private partnerships (PPP, 3P, P3), as business-government collaboration, 150–151

Puerto Rico, deforestation in, 113

Pultegroup, 135, 136*t*

Purina, 90

Q

Quayside, 102

R

Rassweiler, E., 79

Reagan, Ronald, 7n3, 41, 77–78, 79n25

real estate development, as moving toward corporate concentration and power in US, 134

Regional Studies, 106

regulation. *See* government regulation

Remington, 58

rent "burdens," 135, 139, 175

Republican Party (US), 77–78, 189

A Research Agenda for Regeneration Economies (Bryson, Andres, and Mulhall), 171

Restaurant Brands International, 60

retail activity, changes in, 111

Rifkin, Jeremy, 163, 191–192

The Rise of the Creative Class (Florida), 171

The Road to Serfdom (Hayek), 94n29

robocalls, 102

robotic development
    for agricultural use, 114, 115*b*, 116
    impact of, 9
    as part of new technology, 100
    in Pittsburgh, Pennsylvania, 105, 171